THIRD EYE AWAKENING

Discover The Best Techniques to Open Your Third Eye Chakra Experiencing Higher Consciousness, State Of Enlightenment, Expand Your Mind Power, Abilities And Intuition

Table of Contents

Introduction
Chapter 1: The Third Eye
Chapter 2: The Pineal Gland and the Third Eye
Chapter 3: Third Eye Benefits
Chapter 4: Unlocking the Third Eye
Chapter 5: Guide To Discover The Seven Chakras
Chapter 6: Basic Meditation
Chapter 7: The Best Techniques
Chapter 8: Activating the Third Eye through body purification …
Chapter 9: How to Protect Yourself during Third Eye Activation…
Chapter 10: Various Factors That Could Influence The Awakening…
Chapter 11: How To Maintain The Energies
Chapter 12: How To Maintain The Chakras
Chapter 13: Experiences After The Opening Of The Third Eye…
Conclusion

Disclaimer

© Copyright 2021 –All rights reserved.

This book may not be reproduced, or transmitted in any form electronic, mechanical, photocopy, recording, or otherwise, without the prior permission of the author. It is illegal to copy this book, post it to a website, or distribute it by any other means without permission.

Neither the publisher nor the author is engaged in rendering legal or any other professional service through this book. If expert assistance is required, the services of appropriate professionals should be sought. The publisher and the author shall have neither liability nor responsibility to any person or entity with respect to any loss or damage caused directly or indirectly by the professional by using information in this book.

"We have two eyes to see two sides of things, but there must be a third eye which will see everything at the same time and yet not see anything. That is to understand Zen."

D.T. Suzuki

Introduction

There is a fundamental essential force that can be identified in all living beings, according to the ancient traditions of many cultures and religions. The Chinese related to this energy as 'chi' while it is called 'Prahna' in India, and it is named 'Ki' in Japanese culture. Today, several people label this energy from 'life force energy' to 'bioenergy' to 'primal energy' and many more titles. This force is very complex, and scientific research just focuses on being able to measure it. Yet, it can certainly be understood, and its modulation is a key factor in the regeneration of energy to which our body reacts very well.

There are several focus sources in which this force seems to be stored, and our bodies join and exit. Such points are in vortex shape and are called chakras. There are also seven main points in the chakra and several other minor ones. The energy flows through these vortexes with a rotating motion and gives the term, 'chakra' which means 'wheel' or 'that which spins or rotates' in ancient Sanskrit.

At these chakra points, we need to let this normal universal energy move in and out of our bodies to maintain a healthy equilibrium, because when the chakra points are not fully open and revolving, the body can then continue to manifest sickness and pain.

The seven major chakra points are found in our heads or our abstract energy structures or aura, externally at set points. These factors will benefit from being preserved so that the energy will continue to flow, and we can stay physically and mentally healthy.

Growing chakra has its own rhythm, which, by opening and rotating faster with greater ease, can respond to an external stimulus in the form of sympathetic vibrations. The external stimuli which will successfully activate a chakra are mainly colors and sounds. The chakra's pulse itself is very strong, but as each hue has its own spectrum and pitch, and each of the rainbow's seven colors corresponds with each of the chakras ' lower harmonics. Musical notes can also activate the chakras, with a tone once again being a lower harmonic of the chakra's vibration itself.

Growing chakra can basically react to a particular color or musical note. These will also react to other slight vibrations such as natural quartz crystals or other gemstones. Therefore, each chakra has its own corresponding gemstone, which can relax it and help to trigger it.

When we have damaged or rather, one or more of our chakras are not moving at the pace they should be, then our bodies and minds will also be confused, and it may be the source of many other seemingly unrelated physical and mental disorders. Within a second, a qualified energy healer or practitioner will be able to balance the chakras, and this will help the body recover itself on its way. You can also open your chakras and align them with simple meditation exercises.

Here is a very brief overview of each of the chakras with their respective colors and facets.
First Chakra (Root) — Red — Linked to protection and basic energies Second Chakra (Sacral) — Orange— Related to happiness and life Third Chakra (Solar Plexus) — Yellow — Connected to your Emotional Strength Fourth Chakra (Heart)— Green or Pink — Affection and heart problems Fifth Chakra (Throat) — Blue or Turkish — Related to self-expression and contact Sixth Chakra (Third Eye) — Indigo— Cla Chakra (Third Chakra) — It is located right between the eyebrows in the middle of the forehead. It also has a similar location on the back of the head, which also enables a smaller amount of energy to move in and out.

The third eye chakra enables us to get a clear vision of what's going on, and it teaches us to know instinctively, it can also activate our sixth senses with this transparent chakra. The sixth chakra is the ability to come into communication with your own thoughts and recognize your inner self.

Once you open or disable the chakra, you'll find it easy to get in touch with your inner selves. Your perception is stronger as this chakra's relaxation can facilitate the transfer of signals from the brain system that enables the cosmic consciousness to be directly connected. If the chakra is blocked, then all kinds of issues can occur, ranging from insensitivity and the inability to accept new ideas to mental imbalance.

The third eye chakra is aligned with the color indigo and is related to the Silver element. Among others, the gemstone for this chakra is sodalite. Using sodalite can provide a clear understanding that will offer peace and calmness, and also reinforce the nerves. If you need to get rid of old behavior patterns, then this stone can really be a great help when used to open the third eye chakra. As well as dissolving behavior patterns, it also enhances the thinking patterns that we need on a day-to-day basis, giving us more confidence and self-assurance. Achieving rational thinking will support to clear your mind.

Some of the psychological aspects of having a happy or accessible third-eye chakra can be a basic, moral, and mental awakening. It is also believed to improve psychic enhancement and extra-sensorial vision. Nevertheless, if this chakra is out of control, the psychological aspects may manifest in the form of intellectual blockages, shutting off perception, vision denial, and an unwillingness to imagine. Another common symptom of a damaged third-eye chakra is general confusion and headaches.

You can use calming music in key D to align the third-eye chakra yourself. Start visualizing a ball of indigo blue light around the chakra region right in the middle of your forehead. Imagine a stunning Indigo lotus flower as you do this, with two wide petals spreading gradually as it rotates over your chakra. This indigo lotus flower with its two petals reflects the chakra that is described for in the Sanskrit Mandala.

Chapter 1: The Third Eye

The Esoteric Psychic Eye theory and practice have long believed that the psychic eye is the link between the physical and spiritual universe. The spiritual head is more frequently called the "Third Head." The third eye is related to actuarial intuition for the intuitive user and a rise in spiritual awareness. There is an opportunity to "think" as the third eye becomes active, indicating an understanding of the energy fields at higher levels. The third eye vision is not the degree of awareness earthbound correlated with self-identity. When the mind is in a deep state and differs from the body, the third eye is involved.

The third eye traditionally was supernatural. For a long time, the third eye was linked to the skill of intuitive writers. Current science, though, acknowledges that a real physical object is the third eye. It is an organ, known as the pineal gland. From here emerges inner dream. The pineal gland is as small as a pea, deep in the heart of the brain. The pineal gland derives its name from its structure that resembles a very tiny pine cone. The gland is situated behind the head.

The gland releases melatonin, which is related hormonally and has an effect on moods. Gland often affects body biorhythms.

The pineal gland's main activator is the sun. The pineal gland has a similar working relationship to the gland of the hypothalamus. The pineal gland guides the biorhythms while the hypothalamus is the source for vital human needs such as appetite, desire, and our sexual drive. Psychic writers conclude that this gland is a powerful source of heavenly resources.

The mystery concerns third-eye creation or waking for a psychic reading. This isn't mystical, though. The third eye may be awoken, as it occurs in every human. It is a cycle, like any spiritual journey, that requires patience, preparation, and belief. Third-eye stimulation will carry you to a position where you can envision and see beyond what the physical state permits. The third-eye creation would improve psychic abilities for the psychic user.

Third Eye Development

The pineal gland and the pituitary body have to vibrate together to enable the third eye to sense higher dimensions, which is accomplished by contemplation and relaxation. A magnetic field is generated when an appropriate connection is formed between personality, operating through the pituitary body, and the mind, operating through the pineal gland.

Visualization training is the first phase to trigger the third eye by focusing the energies within the inner structure. The magnetic field is formed around the pineal gland by focusing the mind between the pineal gland and the pituitary body on the midway point. The imaginative imagination visualizes something, and this process is given life and meaning by the mind's thinking energies. The creation of the third eye, creativity, and vision are important ingredients in many approaches to differentiate from the physical form. Through the third eye, insight is also obtained. The knowledge and awareness of the astral plane is not recorded in a completely awakened consciousness until the insight is sufficiently strong. Intuition bursts occur with growing intensity as the third eye is triggered to a greater degree by practice.

After closing their eyes, everybody sees patterns or forms, but most of them do not pay attention to the photos because they are not trained to look at images. The photos can come from your higher self, your spirit guides, or other associates with the spirits. It can take time to understand these pictures, but there is no rush.

Some tribal rituals and religious activities refer to the power to see or be mindful of higher energy fields. This abstract perception is much more contextual and does not include the normal level of commonplace consciousness, which mostly includes self-identity. This vision applies to third-eye sight.

The third eye is an organ of the light body that can be called the soul, or etheric body. By opening the third eye, it will have links to the structures or realms of the mind. I apply to the spirit as the mind of a being with color. Such memories include the aspects of history, potential, and current of what some people may describe as time. The third eye is the doorway or portal to space dimensionality, which could be defined as space or time.

To fly, you can reach another world through a gateway. Most people experienced this in part through dreams and visions. Third-eye tuning provides more freedom of choice and transparency for a person.

Third-eye calibration is comparable to cleaning up a camera's lenses. The third eye is thus released from the blockages and debris left by traumas in history, current, potential, and development. Once the third eye is triggered, it is an organ of clear visual contact between the physical body and the light side.

The third eye is generally used by those interested in working for world stability. Your spirit guide directs all of the work.

The third eye is super sensitive, and therefore, moods, diet, drink, and drugs can be easily affected. Some individuals whose third eye is constantly open, appear to be over-stimulated. Such people may find that noise such as television or radio and other electromagnetic devices triggers them discomfort. In these cases, due to over-activity-sensory overload, the third eye is jammed open. This strains the body as it distorts the system of communication of the soul.

You will have a sense of floating in a sea of energy once you have linked with your third eye. Within many societies, this concept is developed through many rituals of contemplation, relaxation, and exercise. Nonetheless, it is not the operation that generates the third eye, meaning that it is the third eye that generates the sense of balance, concentration, attention, synchronization, and flow of your results. The third eye is responsible for the freedom of choice in planning light body activity. The third eye regulates, therefore, the expression of uniqueness and imagination.

The Third Eye is our civilisation's doorway to the future. We will be confronted as a society with recognizing our light bodies as the portion of the soul, responsible for taking charge of the planet earth.

Here's an activity to do.

Sit quietly, clear your head of noise and take a few slow deep breaths, and start focusing your eyes on the computer.

Colors will start to show up. Relax and breathe deeply and gradually, keep watching the colours. The colors now become a form that you may or may not remember.

If you don't see something, this might be because you're not comfortable or because you're anxious. If that occurs, just go out later in the day and begin again.

Physical And Spiritual Qualities Of The Third Eye Chakra

Many people have heard of the "third eye" but have no idea what that means in reality. The word third eye specifically refers to the chakra of the third eye (or brow), or the chakra of the sixth main energetic chakra. It is situated behind and above the two physical eyes, directly in the middle of the eyebrow. In Sanskrit, this chakra is called Ajna, and its color is indigo.

The third eye is concerned with actual physical vision, and when it is out of control (either overactive or underactive), there may be changes in the eyesight of a person or in the field of the body in general, as well as issues with the sinuses, ears, brain, and neck. Spiritually, there may be an overabundance of excessive supernatural experience and knowledge; that is, the awareness of ghosts, the feeling of vibrations, the appearance of metaphysical or mystical manifestations, etc.

(Note: for many psychics and spiritual practitioners, there is no overabundance of these kinds of things—-overabundance means "too much" of something, but once it is fully spiritually and mentally created, all occurrences become incredible. It is through this Ajna or third-eye chakra that individuals psychically experience in the mental or supernatural worlds, be they powers, ghosts, or subtle changes.

A common occurrence that originates within the third eye is what Muktananda and others call "the blue pearl." It is a tiny blue/indigo mark (typically) that appears within the real range of vision of a human. Personally, I see these energetic dots as blue on average, but sometimes they show as gold or white—-no hard and fast law. When these points of light are seen, it usually indicates that the third eye is either opening or shutting; in my opinion, it may also indicate the presence of a real celestial entity (ghost) or power (guide, god, etc.) that would be rare to see without a third eye opened or awoken.

Emotionally, a person lacks awareness and sound perception when the third eye chakra is out of control.

They don't see clearly, be it about the inner or outer stuff, and this can render them frustrated, disoriented, and even violent. Physically, a person can suffer headaches, brain fog, brain tumors, faulty memory, sinus diseases, and more when this chakra is out of control.

When the third eye chakra is balanced and stable, a person can reliably intuit specifics of their climate, circumstances, experienced people, and even future events. Psychic anomalies around an individual also will rise in relation to the third eye's waking and complete working.

If you are actively interested in improving mentally and spiritually, you will usually maintain a keen interest in the energetic chakra network, especially specifically as it affects the third-eye chakra.

Chapter 2: The Pineal Gland and the Third Eye

The center of awareness, the Pineal Gland, is the relation between body, soul, and spirit. It is positioned right behind the eyes in the center of the brain, in a small cave above the Pituitary Gland. The Pineal Gland is very thin, smaller than a pea, in colour; reddish grey and shaped like a pine cone. The Pineal Gland is the organ of the head;it appears like an eye and has all the necessary components for a working body. For pine cone, Pinea is Latin. Pine cone form occurs throughout the ancient world, from the Anunaki and Sumerian ancient most advanced civilizations to the Greek and Roman rituals, to the Vatican and the Papal staff. Throughout ancient Egypt, the pine cone symbolized Osiris' staff. In Ancient days, it was also referred to as the Eye of Horus.

Until very recently, the modern Western medical profession found the Pineal Gland has no particular importance. However, the French scientist René Descartes (1596-1650) stressed the Pineal Gland in his works, naming it the seat of the spirit and the part of the body in which the soul specifically performs its roles.

He said this was the nucleus at which the soul and body were communicating, and where we collect our instructions from the Celestial realms. Years before Descartes, the Greek philosopher Plato assumed that this was our relation to the domains of wisdom and named the Pineal Gland the Eye of Knowledge. It is also considered the mysterious third-eye that is responsible for the spiritual world's mental knowledge and vision. The third eye can see beyond the visible when enabled and becomes the line of communication with the higher planes of being. This has long been known to the Hindus, Buddhist, Taoist, and other ancient traditions in the eastern world, and is now being verified by Western science research.

Through the Pineal Gland we experience higher awareness, often referred to as the God Molecule or the Spirit Gland. After many years of regular therapy, the Pineal Gland is thought to gradually grow in size. In ancient India, the Maharishis were supermen with incredible powers that included generating matter from human energy, telepathy, healing powers that included cell reversal time, invisibility, levitation, interpreting from Akashic history of past and future among other things. Some had Pineal Glands as large as a lemon!

Jesus points to the pineal gland as he says:'The brightness of the body is the pupil, so if your eye is empty, the entire body will be full of light.' Hence he indicated that we should meditate on the pineal gland. Jesus also said:'The people who sat in darkness saw great light.' It indicates that when their third eye was triggered, they saw the light before they were in utter silence. The eye sign is the viewer in truth or our perception distortion.

The crown chakra reaches down until the pineal gland meets the circle. When the Pineal Gland is stimulated, we feel a greater sense of unity and oneness;we gain improved ability to see electromagnetic fields, auras around people and objects, acquire and relay telepathic feelings, pre-cognition of events, and more such phenomena. The stimulation of Pineal Gland plays a crucial role on our road to ascension.

A silver thread binds the astral body through the Pineal gland to the physical body. The small brain region is the source for detecting higher light waves. The higher dimensional light energy that pulsates from the Galactic Nucleus reaches the physical body at the Pineal Gland.

This prana, or vital energy obtained through the energy source in the brain, causes the astral body to vibrate with activity at a higher frequency so that exposure to the divine portal will detach from the physical one. We sense a vibration at the base of the brain when the Pineal Gland is stimulated, and this sensation is often felt when we interact with higher frequencies.

The Pineal Gland, part of the Endocrine System, secretes chemicals including melatonin, serotonin, and dimethyl-tryptamine. Serotonin and melatonin are responsible for our sleep, meditative condition, and physical well-being like relaxation and euphoria. Melatonin is formed by serotonin in the brain, and its development is made possible at night because there is no presence of light. When the light dims or goes out, the development of melatonin, which helps us to sleep starts in the brain, it peaks half through the night and then begins to fall. We need to sleep in total darkness to generate enough Melatonin to increase our overall wellbeing. It is called the DMT or the Spirit Molecule;it can be released while sleep, through divine and supernatural encounters, and during death. DMT, which the brain creates during deep REM sleep, is correlated with the actual supernatural ability of non-physical reality and divine knowledge. I read that, when we're about dying, DMT is also released in extra heavy doses to enable us to review our lives and to make it easier for us to move on. In death, we always hear of people whose entire life was in the form of a short video.

The organ is our instrument of divine perception, our connection between two dimensions, the real and the intangible. This helps us to witness magical and vivid dreams which are important to our spiritual evolution. Some of the hallucinations are signals from the Mind, and antenna built to interpret them is the Pineal Gland. An activated pineal gland can travel purposefully astrally, discover other worlds, predict the future and obtain messages from caring dimensional entities. It also regulates the body's various biorhythms and works in conjunction with the hypothalamus gland, which guides the thirst, appetite, and sexual desire of the body, and the biological clock which decides our aging Some are born healthy with these talents, but others who have underestimated this ability experience none of the unusual extrasensory senses. Through definition, children are usually both intuitive and mystical and can see auras clearly. Yet, most of us lose our expertise as we grow up because of the Pineal Gland calcification.

The big secret to this day is that fluoride present in tap water and toothpaste is the source of this calcification that prevents the spirit world link. Adding to that is consuming processed junk food, drinking soda and other carbonated drinks, white flour, and refined sugars, with minimal values and lack of spiritual practice.

When the pineal gland is activated, we normally experience a lot of improvements in ourselves. We may have sleep problems, our pace of life can change, we may need more or less sleep, and if we can sleep at all, we may have strange hallucinations, psychologically, emotionally, and mentally we go through a chaotic time. We can feel a lot of odd aches and pains, one day low in strength, and high up the next. All of which are natural self-transformation signs, and nothing to think over. The smart thing to do is relax, watch yourself, embrace it, maintain a healthy lifestyle, and maintain a healthy diet. Don't think about it, go with the ride, and let nature take its course. You can accelerate the process by elevating the pulse if you wish. We are human entities, and each of us will have his or her own unique experiences.

According to quantum laws, we are basically electrical entities that live in a state of equilibrium with the earth's electromagnetic field. To activate the third eye and to sense higher dimensions, in order to create a region, the Pineal representing the Spirit and the Pituitary Gland representing the body will vibrate in equilibrium, at yin-yang synchronization. This can be done through reflection, mantra singing, and an ancient Vedic trick, which is looking at the sky. A few of those who have used this approach are Leonardo da Vinci and Nostradamus. All mystical voyages within the domains of the Pineal Gland are reached and observed. Serotonin has the same chemical composition as the hallucinogenic drug. Before you look at the sun with your naked eyes, please inform yourself of the details. It's scary, because you might blind yourself if you don't know exactly what to do, when and how to do it.

We need to clean up our Pineal Gland to be fully operational in order to develop our multidimensional experiences so that it can naturally produce its own DMT to enable us to remain in a creative condition most of the time. DMT is a portion of a medicinal plant in the Amazon called Ayahuasca, which, through its purgative effects, brings deep physical and heart healing and opens the doors to visions of other dimensions. Using water and fluoride-safe toothpaste, eating tamarind fruit, or paste used in preparation is another way for the body to disinfect fluoride. Sauna is just as good too, just sweat everything out of your body. However, as vital as monitoring the dietary intake and maintaining a healthy lifestyle is, nothing overrides the reality that daily spiritual meditation practice, teaching the mind to be still and enabling the healing process to occur naturally are the best ways to reach higher states of consciousness. The calmer you are, the stronger the inward waves, and the more responsive you are to deeper states of consciousness.

There are many ways of stimulating the pineal gland, and it ultimately has to do with air and awareness. The line of consciousness is the silver cord that connects you to the Source through your Pineal Gland. We have bio-electric ways of breathing liquid, and the air is important to the activity of being in the body. With your movement, you are enabled to have an integrated life experience. It influences the endocrine system and the nervous system specifically, as well as the pineal gland, your feelings, your internal thinking, and the entire body. Breathing exercises will actually cleanse the body. Nothing beats a daily meditative spiritual regimen to keep you clean and healthy. Meditation is the best way to stimulate the pineal gland, profoundly and strongly. The product of a regular meditation session is invaluable in all aspects. When stimulating your pineal gland and growing your third eye, it's far more effective than any of the five human senses. You will become conscious of or perceive something that others cannot know, some of the hidden agendas that are going on behind the scenes, and how to make the best possible choices to support you and your children. Your inactive brain functions will get involved. This will help you continue tuning into your seven Higher Senses, and you will be able to use these daily through practice.

Some of the physical benefits identified by practitioners include thicker hair growth, weight loss, and improved weight stabilization, increased energy, and extensive muscle rejuvenation. You can begin to see how the body is also just a process of thinking, and with concentration, you will alter your body more quickly, and you won't have to work out as much. Emotionally, you are trying to go further than your personal problems and the aggravation of everyday life.

The blood will be detoxified, taking old emotional problems to the surface to be removed permanently, so as not to cause disease or harm to the body anymore. You will also feel a restored sense of trust and protection, and extend that to others, enabling you to have more fulfilling relationships, greater loyalty and discernment, and the attractiveness of soul mates. Often, almost all experiences much stronger embodiments of what they want.

The Mystery of the Third Eye

In many ancient religions and mythology, the Mystery of the Third Eye has long been used as an important symbol. The retina, being an organ of sight and hearing, is thought to hold the power to see beyond, or at least, the perception of what is known as reality. The Third Eye is a deeply ésoteric and enigmatic idea that is focused on many beliefs and practices. It is known that a part of the brain called the pineal gland plays a key role in the inner-eye work. The interaction between the pineal gland and the third eye is still being studied to this day, in order to understand its existence and manipulate its strength.

What is pineal gland? One of the most important parts of the endocrine system is the pineal gland. It is found in human and other vertebrates' minds, which resembles a short pine cone (which describes its name). It sits between the two cerebral hemispheres, attached to the third ventricle in the brain's frontal area.

The gland is responsible for producing numerous chemicals, especially melatonin, a serotonin derivative. Melatonin is responsible for regulating the wake-sleep cycle and managing the human body's ability to respond to the seasons. Daylight and darkness affect the gland's ability to produce melatonin. Light that enters the eyes sends signals to the spinal cord, which then stimulates the pineal gland to regulate circadian signals from the body.

Only pineal glands are essential to the normal development of the sexual functions of an organism. Calcification and over-exposure to fluoride and certain drugs, such as anti-depressants, may harm it.

Many authors and experts of psychological research such as H.P. The pineal gland and the third eye Blavatsky also theorized that the 3rd eye is the pineal gland, through its more inactive shape. Because of its position within the brain, it is called a sacred portal or gateway to the human mind and higher consciousness. It was even alluded to by mathematician and philosopher Rene Descartes as the' Seat of the Mind.' It is known in some Eastern religions as the sight by which real awareness can be viewed. It is also believed to be the inner teacher's seat and has often been used as an awakening sign.

The third eye is regarded as the 6th chakra in certain traditions, sometimes depicted as an eye or a spot on the forehead. As such, it is the most important source of spiritual energy that allows the self to recover, increase awareness, and grow. The demon escapes from the physical body through the pineal gland, during astral projection.

Third-eye Activation

The third eye in most people is normally inactive but can be awoken and enabled. This can be achieved with several techniques, including chakra mediation, DMT or intense regression treatment, visualization activities, and kundalini awakening. The last method allows the gradual progression of activation from the chakra located at the base of the spine and up to the chakra in the brow center.

Once this aspect of divine perception is released, the intellect and consciousness of an individual experience considerable change. The open brow chakra encourages intelligence, clarity of thought, increased awareness of self, and the ability to experience a lucid dream. It can also be harnessed to create psychic powers and the Yogic Brain. Basically, what it does is to allow a person to attain their highest potential in enlightened consciousness. You will read more about triggering the third-eye.

It was my keen interest to explore the capacity of human beings, I found a lot of fascinating observations in my work, and if they are true, then we scratch the surface of the larger picture.

Chapter 3: Third Eye Benefits

Opening of the THIRD EYE is the ability to look directly into the universe's dense and enigmatic structure, and into the karmic cause and effect interactions between different people/things. The third eye allows one to look to a certain range in the past, present, and future depending on one's power or depth of meditation and eligibility as controlled by the spiritual master of the person.

1: Higher Awareness— No Pressure, Depression or Worry. Third Eye Meditation With each session, meditation spontaneously moves your mind to higher and higher levels, instantly removing depression and fear from every moment of your life (that is, always!).

Your stress-spiraling fears about how you will compensate for your pending mortgage, student loan, and credit card bills will quickly evaporate.

And will be replaced inevitably by clear and present thoughts about how to be so effective that your pre-meditation iteration appears ridiculous, like looking back at the person you used to be in high school: day and Night.

Finally, with an accessible and active third eye, everything falls into view, the often frivolous concerns of existence go to the wayside. At the same time, you get a clear picture of your real purpose of life— and how to serve it entirely.

2: Acute Intuition: Taking advantage of inner intelligence, opening The Pineal Gland Chakra Through Meditation. Just as meditation has the advantage of reaching higher states of consciousness, which allows you to become more self-conscious, control feelings and juggling effortlessly with the burden of your day, meditation often sets you in a natural-born blessing that we all possess–

Since many traditional cultures believe our instincts to be the most significant 'sound' or 'sight' in our minds, for decades, third-eye meditation has been performed.

As you meditate and become more aware of the amount of the inner wisdom you already have at your disposal, you will want to continue to open and activate your third eye to its fullest capacity.

Better quality, right? The insight into the third eye understands how to fix it. Better Relationship? The intelligence to the third eye understands how to draw. Less job success, and more financial success? The perception to the third eye understands the phase step-by-step. Understanding and accomplishing your real purpose in life? The third eye experience knows exactly why you chose this career.

How much easier will your existence be if your inner-infinite-wisdom resource at your beck and call is accessible? Luckily, the very best solution is sleep.

3: Align with the "Law of Attraction." Manifest the Life You Want, Open Your Eye Chakra With Meditation. We are all human, and while we all want a fear-free life, stressing about how we will accomplish our daily tasks, just perpetuates further anxiety. After all, our thoughts attract like, especially true.

Nevertheless, we continue to have fewer and fewer fears, anxieties, and negative thoughts as we set a time each day to practice meditation, changing the nature of our thinking from the heart. And when they go, what's going to take place will be better and more in line with the universal law of attraction.

When the third eye is gradually opening up, your physical, intellectual, and emotional wellbeing are expanding. In contrast, fresh and higher-level beings are beginning to join your world spontaneously— culminating in new and better ties on all sides.

When your triggered third eye makes the right path to success as simple and visible as the stairway leading to your apartment on the second floor, meditation can allow you to manifest prosperity as easily and naturally as breathing.

4: Seeing what's 'Out There,' Look Inwards: Learning The Right Way with Third Eye Meditation. If you've ever been involved in what's awaiting you 'out there,' but you're not quite sure of what's 'out there,' remember this: there's nothing to dread — anxiety doesn't need to apply.

Some worries you have about your present life, such as what work you will pursue, what decisions you can create in your current relationship, or how you can fulfill your greatest goals and dreams, can all be achieved from the wealth of information found inside thorough meditation.

Meditation allows you to see, grasp, and enjoy the sights and sounds of the previously hidden environment by enabling your third eye, helping you to refine and improve your present life using this enormous reservoir of new information.

Consider the unknown as a seasoned spectator, consider the unlikely probable. The key to unlocking the infinite potential is meditation.

A person's third eye is only under the guidance of one's spiritual lord. If the disciple misuses the power/knowledge gained from the third eye, it can be closed at any time by the spiritual leader who has opened his/her third eye

Only when one is completely mentally renounced (a brahmachari (i.e. a bachelor), or a grihasta (i.e., a married man), though not a sanyasi (i.e., a recluse), has he abandoned all his/her personal desires-i.e. Just selfish desires as selfless interests are fine— to please Him, to improve the world as a whole), and have fully controlled his/her sensual urges— that is, Nutrition needs, scent, contact-physical pleasures-sight and sound and overcome kama-(wishes)andkrodha-(anger/hatred), then the third eye of the human is raised.

If the individual like this is egoless and properly obeys scriptural dictatorships and Master's counsel, then he/she will continue to maintain the influence and also help other common people to solve their personal problems/difficulties in life, making them happy and thus helping to establish justice in society. Such an individual is popular as a great saint.

Many words, smells, touches, and emotions make you feel moody, right? That's just what the goal of sex chakra yoga asana is.

Chakras are in fact the sources of control of the body. Along the spine are seven big chakras. Every chakra is essential for the proper functioning of certain organs, the psychological and emotional dimensions of your existence. Once a chakra is imbalanced or blocked, you can experience symptoms in your mind and body that contribute to back pain.

Apart from back pain, the other form of the damaged second chakra is weak ties. The second female chakras are generally stronger than the men's. Women need this chakra in order to form a new human. If you are a woman and you have problems with relating with other people, most possibly, you have a low sex chakra.

The postures used in yoga are a better way to eliminate back pain, lose weight, and maintain a more flatter stomach. Compared to other types of workouts, yoga asanas are excellent for burning fat and stronger abs, which do not lead to injuries. Yoga poses are very healthy for diabetic patients.

Both yoga poses are health-friendly. After doing standing postures, a person who is always nervous and anxious can feel better, which stimulates the energy of response to the gut-level or the third chakra.

Yoga is used to align the core of energy within the body.

The yoga postures in the first chakra result in prosperity, peace, and fitness.

Yoga postures in the second chakra help to fuel your desires, boost your sexual performance, and hold your emotions in check.

The yoga poses give power and energy in the third chakra.

For the fourth chakra, yoga poses will cultivate sympathy, devotion, and harmony.

You will improve your communication skills and imagination in the fifth chakra.

The sixth and seventh chakras will lead to better vision and spiritual connections, which are opened by meditation and breathing techniques.

Chapter 4: Unlocking the Third Eye

The third eye chakra is often referred to as "Agya Chakra". It is the sixth chakra, and the crown chakra above. This chakra symbolizes intelligence, spiritual strength, insight, and so on. There are several methods for opening the third-eye chakra. Here we'll address the simplest yet very effective meditation technique. Next, find a peaceful place in your house so you won't be distracted during the entire process and can fully focus on your third eye.

1. Close your eyes and move at a steady pace.
2. Drop your head into your chest, and gently begin to breathe until you feel completely comfortable.
3. Now with your eyes closed, attempt to focus with your inner eyes on your third eye region, you can feel like you are looking up without actually opening your eyes.
4. Relax the eyes, and don't push them to face upwards while they are closed. Let them just rest.
5. Do not forget to breathe gentle and easy in the whole cycle because then you only sound clam.

Once you do it daily, you should feel more relaxed gradually and quickly learn the technique of how to unlock the third chakra. Seek to do it every day and in the same position as the mind, body, and soul; get acquainted with the location, and after a couple of minutes, it becomes easy to move easily to a more comfortable level. The mentioned mediation strategy will also help you calm your mind from a full, stressful day.
First, find a peaceful corner in your house so you don't get distracted during the whole cycle and can focus completely on your third eye.

In terms of physical activity, each chakra has a particular role to play, and it influences our personalities. When our chakras are well regulated and transparent, our mental, spiritual, and physical well-being is impaired. Chakra clearance is a great tool for maintaining a healthy living. Many free guides provide a comprehensive step-by-step explanation of chakras, as well as teaching methods for how to unlock each chakra. Chakra principles are not unique and have long been in usage. However, more and more people are interested in upgrading their awareness of Chakra everyday, since this has been proved to be very beneficial by people who have been actively involved in practicing such important methods to achieve intellectual, physical, and emotional health.

Three Common Methods To Open Third Eye Chakra

To open the third eye chakra, which is also called the Ajan chakra predictor of intelligence, insight, and spiritual strength, there are essentially three methods listed below that will help you stabilize the third eye and reap the benefits that such activation provides. These techniques have been attempted for centuries and proved effective in raising the chakra of the third eye.

1. AUM Chanting: AUM chanting uses the sound of seed to activate a common door. This sound affects the middle and activates and unlocks it. Sit up with your eyes closed and sing loudly. Concentrate also on the central chakra while listening to the AUM.

2. Tapping Golden Ax.

The second method of raising the third eye chakra is by using a different technique in breathing. In this method, you divide your inhalations into seventeen sniffs and imagine a silver hammer is hitting the middle of your forehead with each breath. But make sure you keep the whiff so low you can sniff sixteen to complete one inhalation but exhale with one breath. Repeat the process again, and gradually, you can sense your third eye chakra slowly opening up.

3. Alternate Nostril Breathing: Closing your right nostril and taking a deep breath from your left nostril are needed in the third process. Do not hesitate to imagine the air going right from your nostril to your forehead core when you do it. Keep the gas now, then gradually exhale it from the right nostril. Then reverse the process and keep the left nostril inhale closed from the right nostril and then exhale slowly through the bottom.

It is advised that you calm down when you perform it and do not repeat it, as it is a very strong workout, and if you overdo it, you will feel exhausted. Do not push yourself and raise your count gradually.

When our chakras are well regulated and consistent, our mental, spiritual, and physical well-being is impaired. Chakra clearance is a great tool for maintaining a healthy living. Many free guides provide a comprehensive step-by-step explanation of chakras, as well as teaching methods on how to unlock each chakra. People active in the practice of these influential approaches have attained intellectual, physical, and emotional health. Readers are advised to live a happy life by subscribing to different ways of purifying chakras to achieve perfect harmony in life.

Chapter 5: Guide To Discover The Seven Chakras

Chakras are part of the enlightenment cycle of Kundalini, which consists of Nadi, chakra, prana, and Bindu. Chakras are the human body's energy centers where Bindu, the drops of nature, are collected as a result of regulating Nadi, the sources of energy, and prana, subtle light. Once the energy in Chakras is collected, the path to divine perfection is revealed, and the hidden body that lies undiscovered within all awakens.

In every human body, there are seven chakras, not physically, but spiritually, placed just in place of certain glands and organs which control character. The most surprising fact is that, before man invented the terms science, autopsy and organs, these Chakras were examined and discovered long ago. Still today, scientists are curious how older-day people have managed to find Chakras, the body's spiritual centers, and arrange them according to their strength. This is because the glands in or near the location of a specific Chakra lead to the same characteristic of a human being as defined in the Vedas and Upanishads, as the chakras function.

Ajna Chakra-Kundalini Ajna Chakra's last phase to appear is the chakra found right in the middle of our eyes, otherwise named Bruhmadhja. To be exact, the triggering of Ajna Chakra sheds light in the eyes of our subconscious body, the only third eye, and reveals the way to the true Moksha. Kundalini, the rebirth of the unconscious body, is completed shortly after recognizing the distinction between the earth we are living and the other holy universe. Ajna Chakra takes the unconscious body beyond the boundaries of a physical body and reveals where the Divine Discovery finds its next stage before achieving Kundalini's ultimate goal.

Ajna Chakra is at the exact location where a pineal gland, which generates the Melatonin hormone, is situated. The Melatonin hormone is responsible for sleeping and waking, where Ajna chakra takes care of the emergence of the spiritual body going from planet to earth, seeking the truth behind the Divine Being. Both six chakras, except Saharsara, are within human bodies, and Ajna Chakra is the last step to trigger Saharsara and enter Kundalini.

Tilakam-the third eye. A test of an Australian-based animal named Tuatara in the early part of the nineteenth century shocked the scientists involved in the study, discovering a non-functioning but a more identical eye-like component of their foreheads. Further experiments, with this in mind, showed a more surprising finding that the pineal glands are light-responsive; that is, they respond according to the strength of the light and thus release hormones. This truth supports Ajna Chakra's most common name, The Chakra of the Third Eye.

Ajna Chakra is symbolized by two petals, equivalent to the most famous sky shades- violet, gray, and indigo. There is a large inverted triangle, and they all resemble the two dimensions that clash with each other. It is also widely believed that on full moon day and when the lights are more than normal days, the celestial powers and holy spirits come close or down to the planet. This is yet another indication that on special days Ajna Chakra, the third eye, will really see and hear the angels and spirits.

Tilakam, sometimes depicted in lines of three, both vertically and horizontally, in the forehead is a likeness of the third eye found in every human being but lies unseen deep inside our physical body. That's why people are offering Tilakam on long journeys so that the third eye will look after them on their route.
With just the right help from a spiritual guide, who can teach you the way to enable the third eye, through successful activities such as Kriya Yoga, Tantra Yoga, and Kundalini Yoga, the third eye can indeed be discovered inside us!
Some of the world's most misunderstood beliefs, such as Wicca, Witchcraft, Vodou, Tantra, and Vedic Chanting, have real close ties to many of the world's widely spread faiths. To let the people know the differences, the explanations of all the things of theological and cultural significance should first be informed.

Crystal-Healing for the third eye Chakras

A Practical Guide Who really understands chakras amongst us. Much is yet undiscovered, for all that we know about these seven spinal energy sources.
The chakras behave as spinning wheels of light according to ancient texts. Indeed the term chakra is wheel Sanskrit. Chakras obtain and emit energy, whichdepending on the quality of that energy, maybe either negative or positive. You will experience variations in the needs of each chakra during the healing process. You don't need to fear the threat. Think of your chakras as a garden that requires specialized care for every herb. Some chakras need less focus, while others want more attention. The commitment to this self-examination renders it as difficult as it is satisfying to restore the chakras.
The following recommendations may be updated according to the needs. When picking objects, be cautious not about the scale or color but rather about the response when carrying them. Some of these crystals may be alien, but you are likely to find them in a mystical or rock store.

Though this approach to chakra healing may be fun, it is better to undergo long-term therapy with the help of a trained professional. Many skilled chakra healers are extremely intuitive, as well as qualified. Their analytical perspective can help you understand why each imbalance is induced. That in and of itself can be soothing.

1st Chakra: This chakra is heart. It is at the root of your neck, or tailbone. The root chakra is a part of the physical world. If in the present you feel anchored, safe and rooted, the chakra requires no care. Many aren't that lucky, though. A blocked root chakra can cause you to understand the physical and become overly possessive and clingy. Conversely, you can sound strangled from your body and belongings when you are too free here. As a consequence, they will take advantage of your hospitality.

Crystal Correction: The obsidian unlocks a damaged chakra. This jewel provides a centric, calm outlook so that an appreciation of the temporary nature of possessions eliminates the desire to accumulate compulsively. Place a piece of obsidian on your genital area when lying on your back to repair cracks. When you relax more, the power of the stone can interact with your own;it will strengthen. An abundantly accessible root requires rose quartz. A soft pink quartz, while typically associated with the head, helps us to embrace and enjoy ourselves, so we can defend ourselves by saying no

2nd Chakra: The sacral chakra governs our sexual energy and creativity. Just click two inches under your navel to know the position. A happy sacral chakra is an offering of expressiveness and flourish. A blockage may contribute to resistance to new ideas. In the "drama queen" as well as in other reckless behavior, from bed-hopping to dangerous driving, a sacral chakra which is too exposed is apparent.

Crystal Correction: Carnelian, this quartz type is perfect for the sacral field to expand. Although it can be seen in many colors, the calming red or orange properties offer shy confidence. This helps us to fulfill our goals, without fear-based perceptions that obstruct our path. Conversely, if this chakra is too accessible, lapis luizi may be needed. In ancient Egypt and Babylon, this traditional light blue stone was highly valued. Today we may take advantage of its moderating powers to help us behave with caution.

In Quartz, Jewels & Metal Spells, Scott Cunningham writes: "Touching the body with this stone literally strengthens the intellectual, physical, moral, psychological, and emotional health." Rest this stone as long as possible for maximum benefits to the 2nd chakra.

3rd Chakra: This is the solar plexus, also known as the control core. This is where a pool of untapped will and courage remains. When this chakra is safe, we realize our ability and are inspired to pursue it. We may have "butterflies in our gut" while trapped, or we may experience certain stomach troubles. A blocked center of control is making us behave and feel powerless. When this energy-center is too small, the opposite problem happens.

Crystal Correction: Golden Beryl is a soft, yellow lemon stone that guides will and increases confidence. Consequently, blockages for the 3rd chakra are awesome. Placing this stone two inches above your navel can unlock your power center and help you make your goals come true. Green jade is for those who are confused by this Chakra. The calming stone serves to subtly and harmlessly direct our emotions, and eliminates destructive thoughts to others.

4th Chakra: This is the chakra of the heart, and the location thereof is self-explanatory. This is the domain of spiritual growth, devotion, strength, and high ideals in the divine. A congested chakra in our core renders us excessively critical of both ourselves and others. We find it hard in this state to give ourselves up to possibilities of love and friendship. Conversely, if our heart is too heavy, we might seek to do the unthinkable, trying to carry the world's weight.

Crystal Correction: The green jasper, put on the face, allows us to feel secure enough to open up and reveal ourselves. It encourages contact frankly and with pleasure. Seek peridot for a core that has no limits. The soft, pastel-green stone refreshes us and also calms us down. Peridot helps us to be caring, and not selfish.

5th Chakra: The chakra of the throat allows us to connect through language as well as physical. It's situated at the throat foundation. We speak honestly and freely when this chakra is healthy. If we stopped here, then our deception is fragile.

We might, for instance, leave out details. Instead, if this chakra is expanded, we're communicating too much and without preconceived reasoning. This is generally called the condition of "foot in the ass."

Crystal Correction: Sodalite, a lovely navy crystal, helps with chakra of constricted throat. The stone brings us insight and confidence. We can make that with certainty, knowing our facts. Those with a large 5th chakra, on the other side, need to make their reality weaker. Amber is supportive in this capacity. This stone is soulful and deep. Kevin Sullivan states in The Crystal Handbook that "Amber represented the resting place of the spirit(s) thought to inhabit the stone in Viennese mystic literature." Fossilized, multimillion-year-old tree sap, amber provides us with early earth's natural knowledge.

6th Chakra: This energy source, situated between the brows, is recognized by many as the third eye. That chakra, if in harmony, gives us the ability to see the past sight, exposing our inherent spiritual skills. But, when it's stopped, we restrict ourselves to evidence that has not been investigated. This contributes to rigid thinking and happiness, which is disrupted.

But if we're too transparent here, we might get separated from the physical world. The unwillingness to close the psychic eye fills with a perturbing feeling of unreality as necessary. Equilibrium is essential. We also have to wake up Crystal Correction when we dream: a moonstone put on the 6th chakra will clear up the problems that hinder our instincts and open the mind to the unknown. Since moonstone is linked to cycles of transformation, it is an invitation to personal growth. This allows us to turn in wind, to allow spontaneity and to break rigidity. Blue lace agate is required, with an overly open 3rd eye. A stunning, sky-blue stone sharpens our attention and removes the fog of emotional interference.

7th Chakra: Awake! Terms are not enough to convey the crown chakra's power. This chakra is situated at the top center of your brain, which offers the prospect of enlightenment. Though juggling, it will not render us a Buddha, it will surely bring us to the heights of divine bliss and bind us to the meaning of our lives. You are far from alone if you're stuck here. A good chakra to the crown is unusual. It is the blessing of tireless efforts in the creation of the spiritual self. We may be uncertain about our future while interrupted and miss permanent, rapturous calm. We must first maintain the well-being of our previous chakras for maximum results at maintaining this chakra. It's unusual to have this chakra too accessible unless you hate peace and harmony. And we stay among the disillusioned. We have to be able to communicate with the cynic as well as the sorry. Otherwise, we will be stuck within our own heads. It can get pretty lonely as secure as this place is.

Crystal Correction: Transparent quartz for all chakras is a trustworthy healer, but it is particularly useful in opening the closed crown. The chosen crystal should be tiny enough to sit on the top of your head, due to the location of the 7th chakras. This stone offers clarity of purpose in everyday events and helps us to see the broader meaning. In doing so, it helps us to understand the universal truths and function by harmony. Hematite is the treatment for those with an excessively exposed crown chakra. It is healing, too. Through drawing attention to the practical realities of life, this mysterious, strong stone will help us fulfill our own worldly needs and those of others.

Sidebar: Find your obstacles with a pendulum. Use a pendulum to treat the chakra imbalances quickly and reliably. Get a 6-sided quartz pendulum out of a rope or chain to launch. Such beauties are held in many mystical stores. Steadily keep this stone over the chakra that you're most concerned about. You'll soon notice the crystal is beginning to move. Don't be concerned about the swing course. Alternatively, depth is what counts. The vast swing suggests the unnecessarily open chakra, where a compact, unstable swing defines the block.

Chapter 6: Basic Meditation

Chakra meditation is a perfect way of improving your spiritual well-being. You shift your focus by doing chakra meditation. Not only do you feel better when you change your attitude, but it can also help you move forward more quickly on your journey.

That's why meditation on chakras can be perfect for you when you feel confused somewhere. Holding the energy healthy and moving lets you get linked to a higher vibration point. Your Self and the World (God, Higher Origin, etc.) interact more readily as the world does not have to go through all the metaphysical muck produced in your energy system.

A Short Description of Chakras and Chakra Meditation

The term chakra means "bar" or "disk" in Sanskrit. These are spherical, funnel-shaped sources of energy that are believed to be found within the etheric source of reality often called the subtle body.

The etheric body is the non-physical body that our real bodies are superimposed over. It is an exact duplicate of our physical body but in a shape of greater energy. It can be calculated as the electromagnetic fields in and around everything.

The chakras transfer energy into the body. We even transmit the pulse of our feelings, desires, and physical health into the energy field around us. Looking at a person's chakras and aura will give you a glimpse of what they might experience or how well their thoughts and physical bodywork, if you can see it psychically.

I've noticed the difference my students can make in chakra meditation on the energy system. When I teach people to do chakra meditation, there is a tangible difference I can sense in their energy and sometimes in the room's energy from before and after meditation on the chakra. Psychically I can see the gap in their chakras before and after. Most usually, the chakras are symbolized as cones of whirling energy or petalled flowers. Chakras have openings in both the front and back of the etheric structure, except the crown (pointing up) and core (pointing down) chakras with one gap.

Chakras Used in Traditional Meditations

These are the ones that most mp3s rely on chakra meditation. The first chakra, the Root Chakra, binds us to the earth and is about our roots and kin. That too, is where we feel safe and secure because we are healthy and on our feet.

Common name: Root Chakra, Core Chakra Sanskrit name: Muladhara (meaning Support) Location: Spine core, Perineum. The Root Chakra is a red sphere of energy pointing down towards the Moon. The red is visualized as bright and vibrant as possible in a chakra trance, which reaches down from the perineum between the knees.

The second chakra, the sacral chakra, is correlated with the influence of feminine energy (both in males and females) and imagination.

Common name: Sacral Chakra, Splenic Chakra (this chakra is situated above the spleen in some Eastern systems) Sanskrit name: Svadhisthana (meaning sweetness) Location: Lower abdomen, around two inches below the navel. The sacral chakra is orange in color. There are two cones of electricity-one that falls out in the body's face, and one in the body's back. You should think of a perfectly ripe orange in a chakra visualization to help you imagine the beauty of the orange color.

Solar Plexus Chakra The third chakra, the chakra of the solar plexus, is the core of strength, center of personal power, self-esteem, and self-worth. It's the same place where you get that innate intuitive feeling or subconscious intuition.

Common name: Solar Plexus Chakra Sanskrit name: Manipura (meaning Lustrous Diamond, or Jewel of the Navel) Location: Solar plexus, upper abdomen, under breastbone, about two inches above the navel. The solar plexus chakra is bright yellow. It has two energy cones, one in the back and the other in the forehead. Dream about the light in a chakra trance, and how bright yellow it is. That's how vividly you want your solar plexus chakra to be visualised.

The fourth chakra, the chakra of the head, is where we keep affection-for others and ourselves. Compassion and pardon grow here. Loving connects us with others and with the world.

Common name: Heart Chakra Sanskrit name: Anahata (meaning Unbeaten or Unstuck) Location: Chest core. The heart chakra is marked as emerald green or purple. It has two energy cones, one in the back and the other in the forehead. Whether pink or green is ok in a chakra meditation. None is stronger than the other. That's what is resonating with you.

The fifth chakra, the throat chakra, is about the ability to express yourself, to be imaginative, and to connect. This chakra is linked to spiritual perception or clairaudience.

Common name: Throat Chakra Sanskrit name: Visshudha (meaning Purification) Location: Center of the throat. The throat chakra is blue sky. It has two energy cones, one at the back and one at the front. You want to turn the color a warm sky blue or the blue you see in the Mediterranean waters in a chakra trance. Sorry, no baby blues and no pastels.

Third Eye Chakra six is our source of inner vision, creativity, and insight. That's where we can control clairvoyance or seeing the paranormal.

Common name: Third Eye or Brow Chakra Sanskrit name: Ajna (meaning Perceive or Command) Location: Center of the forehead (not center of the eye brows). The 3rd eye chakra is indigo. It has two energy cones, one in the back and the other in the forehead. Think of the midnight-blue sky in a chakra trance to help you with the indigo light.
Crown Chakra
Chakra seven, the crown chakra, binds us to the higher self, the greater consciousness, and the universe's spiritual knowledge.
Common name: Crown Chakra Sanskrit name: Sahasrara (meaning Thousand-fold or Thousand-Petalled lotus) Location: Top of head, slightly forward. The crown chakra is decorated in violet, gold, or silver. There is one capacity cone that extends inward.

Why are Chakras being Clogged Up?

You are an offensive person. Your feelings and ideas are resources too. Chakras get clogged with dark-looking, sluggish, intense energy when we have thoughts and emotions full of self-criticism, prolonged rage, prolonged shame— all the destructive forms of energies we normally try to avoid slipping into.
Your physical body too will influence how your chakras work. Your feelings, emotions, and physical health are commonly believed to be all intertwined.
I've seen sick people with a turbid, thin, tiny, and gloomy energy system. I also saw chakras in different health problems-from being small and usually vibrant to curiously made, bland in color, immense and shiny, cold and depressed, dark, and heavy feelings. These are all manifestations of the state of mind, desires, and physical health of the person. Unpleasant feelings, healthy eating, heat, being surrounded by negative people, all of these factors will begin to affect the quality of your energy frequency.
Those appear to be lower quality, smaller energy waves that can be processed or integrated into your energy system. When that occurs, it begins to affect how the chakras will store water. That's when chakras get clogged up and may start blocking themselves.

Why Chakra Meditation Works

Chakra Meditation makes use of your mind's control and the ability to envision shifting nature. Energy will influence the mind.
Chakra therapy helps you stay focused on your mind and takes you through every chakra. In meditation, you are directed to perceive any chakra.
Sometimes I have students who are having trouble seeing or are trying to open up their clear-sighted skills. This is perfect because you can't psychically see your chakras.

You do not need to be successful for you to have chakra meditation. I ask my students to feel in these situations, visualize what they think their chakras look like, or just wonder what that specific chakra is.

You think that's perfect too. In clearing your chakras, it is the purpose and concentration that is essential.

The meditation on chakras that I offer to people can be performed every day or anytime you need to. You don't even need to use the mp3 anymore once you get into the flow, although some people really like being driven through it.

When you notice there is one specific chakra that is more difficult to visualize or takes longer to clear, that implies there is a certain barrier in that field of energy. Sometimes it is a conviction we cling quite stubbornly about ourselves or the universe. Some days it's because we usually ignore our own needs for comfort and recovery.

If you have difficulty visualizing the light, you might want to pick up some colorful chips of paint, one for each chakra hue, and have it with you for contemplation on the chakras. You can use them as a guide.

There are other methods for removing the chakras and aura that I teach in my lessons. I always teach people to have healthy emotional boundaries so that they don't get as much attention from other cultures as they do.

I do believe; however, that your mind is the most powerful and useful resource that you have and that doing chakra meditation is a fast, efficient and quick way to keep your chakras in good working order.

Important Rules For Utilizing Chakra Meditation

There are many different kinds of methods in meditation out there, and one of these is a meditation on chakras. Chakras of meditation use different points inside the body center to regulate certain areas. When correctly employed, this form of meditation can be a powerful tool for treating sickness, body disorders, but also for fostering general well-being. We don't know the first thing about Chakras for many, though, or use them in meditation, so here are few basic tips to support you with this kind of meditation.

The first thing you will need to do is get familiar with what the Chakras are and to understand the power of this practice. Seven chakras travel up the spine, from the base of the spine up to the top of the head. The term chakra means wheel of light, so if you could really see them, seven light wheels would be located in the middle of your body.

While it would take more time for the topic of what chakras are and what each wheel depicts, here are the basics. The first chakra is called Muladhara, the root chakra, and it is located near the tail bone at the base of the spine. It is shown in red. It is the chakra that gives us Mother Earth. This is the chakra, which helps us to make things manifest in the real world.

The second chakra, or sacral chakra, is the Svadisthana. It is under the belly button and is portrayed by the orange color. This is where imagination finds its way. This chakra is the corporeal, mental nucleus.

The third chakra is the Chakra Manipura, the solar plexus. It is located just below the bone of the breast, centering behind the stomach. This is where there are pride, desires, and rage. There you are always sensitive to spiritual guides and psychological growth.

Anahata is the fourth chakra, found near the shoulder blades behind the breastbone. This is the chakra of the heart and is depicted in purple. It is the source of devotion, kindness, and spirituality. This binds the body and mind too.

The throat chakra, the fifth, is classified as Vishudda, or throat chakra, and is located at the neck root. It is light blue. That's where there's touch, voice, writing, and even sounds.

The Ajna is called the Sixth Chakra, or the Third Face. It is located in the middle of the forehead, just above the lips. This wheel is indigo and is the source of insight, divine energies, and intuitive powers.

The seventh chakra, the crown chakra is Shasrara, right at the top of your mouth. This is expressed with the violet color. This is where you're finding complex emotions, strength, and enlightenment.

Essentially, the various chakras represent different parts of your body, and they can become out of sync just like the actual parts of your body. Concentration on one aspect above all else will focus energy more on one chakra than another, which effectively knocks the others out of balance. Though these are a metaphysical phenomenon, they have a great deal to do with manipulating the body's physical world.

For one chakra, too much energy will cause problems that you may not even be conscious of. Let's take the root chakra for one case, Muladhara. This is where doubts are heard. In the negative emotion, a lot of energy is used, which can throw this chakra out of whack. This implies you'd have an enormous amount of fear, but the other six's still depleted resources. If you're out of sync with the chakras of your body, you can feel anything from unexplained anxieties, body aches, and pains, or even mental illness.

On the other side, maintaining a balanced chakra force brings you a greater sense of well-being, being able to accomplish everything set before you, and being able to help keep away physical ailments, as mind, spirit and body are attuned to each other.

So you have a great tool to help you remain calm and concentrated by using chakras meditation. This binds you to the sky, but it leaves you rooted as well. You will cure yourself physically as well as emotionally, by using yoga chakras to hold your whole being in harmony. You will find out much more from a variety of sources on this form of meditation.

You can go online, or you can find books, charts and more tips here if you have a metaphysical shop in your town.

Making Chakra Meditation a Big Part of Your Life

Meditation is one of the best things you can do to make your mind, spirit, and even your physical body feel a little better. It is a tradition that has been with us for thousands of years; India's ancient civilization was one community fully aware of the benefits of meditation. We in the West have only gradually come to understand meditation as a method for achieving better mental and spiritual wellbeing. Chakra mediation is one of the most efficient and basic forms of meditation (and the most common for precisely this reason).

The Principles of Chakra Meditation
 Chakra Meditation is a way to strike a balance between the body's seven energy centers, these are called Chakras. Once these energy centers are properly balanced, it is possible to achieve the optimal flow of energy through the body. Some seven Chakras should be clarified briefly:
1. The Crown Chakra — located at the top of the head, is the Chakra that pertains to our thinking; intelligence, awareness, and our very consciousness.
2. The Brow (or Third Eye) Chakr — this Chakra is situated between the eyebrows and is connected to the aspect of light, i.e., our vision and imagination abilities.
3. The Chakra of the Throat — this Chakra is located at the base of the throat and is connected to the sound function. This Chakra is linked to our communication skills and our imaginative urges.
4. The Chakra of the Heart — found close to the heart in the middle of the chest, this Chakra is responsible for your ability to love and feel compassion and to rule your relationships. This Chakra is connected to air dimension.
5. The Chakra Solar Plexus (or Strength) — situated just above the navel, this Chakra is linked to our strength of will and our metabolism as well. This Chakra is connected to the fire dimension.
6. The Holy Chakra — found just below the navel, this Chakra is connected to physical love and our generative organs, as well as the artistic instinct.
7. The Root (or Foundation) Chakra — Found at the base of the spine; this Chakra is responsible for our overall physical wellbeing, protection, and wealth as well. This Chakra is connected to the Earth dimension.
Nothing works better than Chakra practice to reset yourself and bring things back into proper balance. If all these essential centers of energy are balanced correctly, you will enjoy better health — physical, mental, and spiritual. Meditation with chakras will make a huge difference in promoting better health and a better life.

The Chakra Meditation method comprises of three techniques:

1. Grounding-This strategy is aimed at making you feel physically rooted to Earth. Close your eyes and see a seed rising from your body down into the Earth below you. In order to do that effectively you will need to work intensively.
2. Centering Strategy-Take several steps back. Tighten and loosen every part of your body, from top to bottom; imagine yourself as comfortable as you do. Ultimately, imagine one piece of pottery centering on the wheel of a potter.
3. Relaxation strategy-This can be anything that helps to create the desired state of relaxation for you, but many consider that the strongest methods for simulation are to do this.

Here's a simple way to do chakra meditation:

A) sit in a comfortable spot, or lie down.
B) Close your eyes and start turning off external stimuli-you want as little triggers as you can.
C) Breathe naturally; your air will of course hit the right state.
D) Start concentrating on every part of your body from your toe to your eyes. Arms still closed, sense the floor on which you sit or lie, the breeze around you; imagine your surroundings.
E) At first, you will find this difficult, but just let some intrusive thoughts run through your mind-they'll sort out themselves and vanish with practice.
F) Do not hold back your consciousness; let it pass through your blood, as it will.

Do this meditation at any time of the day, as long as necessary!

5-Minute Chakra Meditation

This is a basic five-minute chakra meditation that is fast enough for those who are just starting meditation but can also benefit those who are used to more advanced techniques. This workout helps to balance / align the seven big chakras all over the body. In addition to calming the chakras, certain additional benefits of this rapid exercise involve, but are not limited to:

- Lower blood pressure
- Improve concentration
- Regulate your heart rate
- Relax your nervous system in a stressful situation
- Enhance blood flow and oxygen levels in your mind and body
- Help to alleviate both physical and emotional pain

This conviction goes back to ancient India and the term chakra comes from the Sanskrit word ' oven.'

The idea that energy flows through these seven main chakras providing well-being and physical, mental, and spiritual wellbeing to those whose chakras are properly balanced. If one or more of those chakras are not properly balanced / aligned, the body, mind and spirit will not perform as well as it should. During your busy day, this fast meditation can be used to get your energy centers (or chakras) back into alignment that will help you to succeed in everything you do.

With any meditation it is best to relax and get relaxed in a nice, quiet area. This is not always necessary, though, and I used this practice in the doctor's office, the softball games of my friend, in restaurants where people screamed... You get the photo. Let's just have fun!

Take a minute first, then start breathing. Close your eyes, and just count every intake. Inhale deeply and release oxygen while counting "five." Inhale slowly, release and mark "two" When you get back to four continue at "three."

Only concentrate on counting your intake and erase those emotions softly when they enter your mind.

This is a simplified version of breath counting and it only requires about 45 seconds to one minute to do this.

When you concentrate on your breath, you can sense your body already beginning to relax. We will now work our way up your chakras, taking about 30 seconds on each one. Picture a rotating colorful disk (or wheel) in each respective area as you concentrate on each specific chakra.

The first chakra, the Foundation or Root Chakra, is located near the tail bone foundation, and is defined by the red color. When you breathe visualize a red disk rotating at the base of your tailbone, or "bar." You should be more comfortable and you're going to want to spend more time on each chakra, but 30 seconds can work if a busy schedule allows for that.

The second chakra, the Sacral Chakra, is about one inch below the navel, and is defined by the orange colour. Consider this time an orange disc revolving an inch below the navel but over the first chakra.

Gently remove any other concerns than this revolving orange light, breathing deeply yet gently. Enable 30 seconds before continuing again.

The third chakra, the Solar Plexus Chakra, is in the (you know it!) region of your solar plexus, or just below your breast bone. This chakra is depicted in the color yellow so picture a yellow spinning disk near the bottom of your throat. While you're doing this quickly visualize spinning all three together as if on a loop.

These first three chakras are aligned with our physical body and our connection and communion with Mother Earth, and represent it. The top three chakras in turn associate you with your mental state and higher spiritual selves. For this reason many people find the fourth chakra to be the most critical of the seven chakras. The Heart Chakra, with the top three chakras, transcends the bottom three and retains the essential equilibrium between both.

When you step into the Chakra of the Heart, sense your body is starting to relax and just concentrate on your heart.

Breathe deeply, and concentrate on a rotating green disk above your core. Feel free to take a few extra moments with this Chakra and welcome the change from your physical needs to your inner aspirations. Most people are having a hard time with this move but it becomes easier with practice.

Starting from the Chakra of your heart, embrace the change from your human being to your spiritual self. The next chakra is in your chest, and is defined by the blue color. When you breathe deeply imagine the movement of a blue disk in your throat reflecting your Throat Chakra. Taking in the serenity as you prepare to move into the sixth chakra.

Take a calming breath and move up to the Third Eye Chakra in the middle of your forehead. When you breathe visualize the movement of an indigo colored disc in the field just above your head. Only concentrate on your revolving chakra and visualize it opening and making the energies flood in.

Now move up to your heart, or your Crown Chakra, and imagine the spinning of a brilliant violet disk. The chakra is exposed when you relax and imagine a rotating disk and the electricity passes through your body. You should get the sensation of increased energy at this stage as well as a relaxing aura throughout the body.

When you take these final breaths, the force passes through your chakras and out of your Chakra Cap. Take in the sensation, not just in your mouth, but around you.

An exercise lasting five minutes can be performed almost anywhere or at any time to help increase energy whilst relaxing the mind and nerves.

Are there any dangers of practice with the Chakra?

Should one be taking precautions while doing meditation with chakras? This method of therapy is often practiced in sessions involving Yoga and Reiki. Chakra practice works on the seven main chakras from the base to the top. Another style of meditation, similar to Kundalini Yoga, will create strong currents of energy that travel up the spine, energizing chakras along the way. Although meditating on the chakras that produce feelings of peace and consciousness, in certain circumstances there is some controversy about its health.

Contraindications for chakra meditation In fact, chakra meditation is considered safe when done gradually with proper guidance. Nonetheless, anyone with the following conditions can stop meditation of this sort, unless they are closely supervised by an experienced teacher in meditation.

- Epileptic seizures
- mental or emotional disorders
- heart disease and other serious physical problems
- drug treatments Possible effects of chakra meditation

Chakra meditation induces physiological and psychological improvements in the mind, body and spirit. Maybe unintended side effects, such as the following symptoms, can arise when done incorrectly or without proper guidance from a professional meditation or yoga teacher.

- Shivering along the neck
- feelings of electricity running through the body
- sudden muscle motions
- pain or vomiting
- shifts in breathing habits
- laughing or crying spontaneously
- auditory or visual disturbances
- fear, disorientation or agitation
- responses to distorted memories
- out - of-body encounters
- changed sleep cycles
- enhanced intellectual capacity In spirit
- Opening the chakras provides an opportunity to get in contact with the dark energies hidden inside the body, also generating spiritual experiences and feelings of harmony with the universe.

Some meditation experts believe that poor meditation encounters are more likely to occur when the individual doing the meditation is under a lot of stress, has long-term difficulties or has blocked past memories, or is doing the practice without a well-trained guide's support and help. Anxiety of meditation on the chakras or unrealistic perceptions can also lead to bad experiences. Anyone who has these signs will contact a competent psychiatrist or health care professional who is experienced with these issues.

When used properly to remove blockages in the energy fields of the body, this type of meditation will help prevent illness, enhance mental and emotional health and lift the mind to a deeper level of consciousness.

As a form of meditation for the healthy mind, body, and spirit-soul Chakra is the secret to physical health, emotional stability, and intellectual clearness. This is because our chakras act as conductors, extracting energy from the heavens and the earth to unify them.

Chakras are simply tourbillons of electricity. The fusion of those forces is what makes a chakra. It is a whirlwind of moving force, which then activates various endocrine organs within the body to secrete hormones into the bloodstream. Chakras are represented as a kind of funnel inside that funnel, with smaller funnels. They are often identified as lotus flowers too. The ingestion of individual chakras has also been intuitively interpreted by many as being identical to the blades of a fan or windmill that rotates in circular motion. Chakras are doors that allow the flood of our prana-life energy in our aura. Our central purpose is to vitalize the physical body, and to promote our self-awakening.

We are connected to human, mental and emotional staff. There are seven big chakras which are known universally.

In fact, the aura is known as the eighth chakra. Indeed our first chakra (root) stretches outside of the body. It's located between the legs... between the elbows and the physical body about half way. The seventh chakra, regarded as the crown chakra, is above the ear. The remainder of the chakras are distributed sequentially along the back, arm, and skull (sacral, solar plexus, heart, mouth, and eye). Individually, the chakras mimic funnels with openings close to petals. While chakras are not visible to the human eye, skilled subtle-energy staff may interpret them psychically.

The Importance of Chakra Meditation

Getting a knowledgeable and experienced person qualified in subtle-energy work studied and handled the chakras is a great way to learn how the body functions on a metaphysical level. Metaphysical energy practitioners skilled in chakra yoga will inform you which of the chakras are in poor condition, which ones are overworked, and what you can do to relieve this pressure.

For e.g, if the chakras perform at a lower level, the remainder of the chakras will be forced to pick up the slack. In reality, non-functioning chakras will "blow out" an otherwise safe chakra which obviously isn't pleasant. By example, one will take a trip to the chiropractor's clinic for an improvement when the ones back or hip go out of sync. Similarly, a mystical energy worker qualified to control the flow of energy will allow one to have misaligned chakras changed back to working order. A few sessions with a healing practitioner may be required to get energy levels back to speed. You can then take a variety of health activities to help keep the chakras open and working optimally, enabling natural flow of your energy.

Best Methods of Chakra Meditation

I've learned that mantra practice is the best way to balance and heal through chakra meditation. Learning to work within the chakra domains with your' telekinetic' mind power is incredibly effective and strong. So in the sense of chakra meditation I think everyone should learn to work with telekinetic energies. Maybe it's so powerful because telekinesis also known as' PK' is a scientific fact that has been proved consistently at leading universities around the world and by top scientists around the world. And, Chakras are also a scientific fact, as the oldest mapping system of human development, wellbeing and behaviour!

My preferred form of yoga is Bhakti and it has the most powerful effect of holding them in the best shape on the chakras. And although my Bhakti practice isn't great, it's still incredibly beneficial in my life! The practice of matra and vegetarianism is very purifying, and it really does almost inevitably make a world of difference. The bottom line is that operating within the chakra realms allows you to take charge of your universe. It's so easy. All you need to do is take the next step, to study the most effective techniques of chakra meditation. Chakras are also a scientific fact and therefore they are so successful in resolving areas of our lives that need help with recovery,' massage,' and/or subtle-energy.

How does chakra music function in meditation?

By using music for chakra meditation, you can quickly relax the chakras in a faster and easier way than just meditating.
The music of chakras meditation uses binaural beats. Such beats are extremely effective, because they are aimed at activating all 7 chakras.

Such beats activate the 7 chakras by causing different levels of sound energy into every brain. In these rhythms, the difference in frequency ranges lets all of your 7 chakras work and open at incredible speed. The effect is an immense stream of energy that makes you feel full of life and vitality.

Using chakra calming music or binaural beats doesn't have any side effects and once you start using them you can quickly feel a change in yourself and your meditation experience.

Your meditation session will be much richer and more relaxing, and when you're finished you'll feel much more re-energised. You'll sense the vibration flowing through your chakras, literally.

Chakra mediation music has confirmed performance, which is why more and more people perform chakra meditation on a daily basis using chakra meditation music and rhythms.

It is important to understand that specific frequencies activate each of the 7 chakras. This implies that while one level of sound will activate one of your chakras, it will have no effect on the others.

That's why it's so crucial to use binaural beats; because it's an essential tool to attune and align your chakras.

I got mails from readers who wanted to relax and align their chakras with meditation alone. In this pursuit they spent years and later tried binaural beats. They tell me they wish they did it earlier and that after using these beats their mediation sessions were incredibly different and much deeper. In reality, they're the ones who inspired me to start meditating with binaural beats and I use them daily now.

This is to experience the benefits of contemplation on chakra balance and the feeling of well-being as quickly as possible.

Chapter 7: The Best Techniques

A person may use many different meditation techniques. The important thing is to find a form in therapy that you are familiar with, and try to stick to it. When you continue to jump from one meditation technique to the next you won't get all the benefits of meditation. Meditation has many physical, neurological and moral advantages to it. Some of these involve lower blood pressure, better skin tone, a happier look at life, less pain, and a sense of well-being overall. Today we'll also give a brief summary of five of the main meditation techniques.

Trataka - The first meditation method we want to explore is the meditation treataka. In Sanskrit Trataka means looking or staring. An individual fixes his or her eyes upon an external object while practicing Trataka Meditation. This can be a spot on the ground, a burning candle or anything. Trataka Meditation is an ancient discipline performed for the production of focus and the Ajna chakra (third eye). The person basically gazes at the target until the eyes start watering. They let all emotions float into their heads as they look and pass away. Once the eyes start weeping then the eyes are closed.

If Trataka Meditation is done with a candle after the eyes start weeping and the individual concentrates on the vision of the flame being extinguished. This will be a picture after image at first but will fade into seeing the image with the lens of the minds. This is a safe way to develop the Chakra of the third eye.

Chanting- The next method for contemplation is mediation by chanting. Mantra Meditation is the position where you say a word like ohm in your head over and over. The word works like a car in Mantra Meditation which brings you to a state of no thinking. It is very natural for the mind to wander off into other thoughts while repeating the mantra or the word. When this occurs the individual needs to bring his thoughts back to the slogan of gentleness and start repeating it again. In mantra mediation the repeated word is unique for the purpose of spiritually changing the individual. A mentor may usually convey a quote to a meditator.

Chakra - The third method of meditation is concentration on the Chakra. The human body is composed of seven big chakras. The individual should concentrate on a particular chakra while practicing Chakra Meditation for the purpose of healing or energizing the chakra. Chakra Meditation is capable of revitalizing a person's body through the cycle of healing and revitalizing it. It is best to begin with the root chakra as the chakras are interrelated and work your way up while practicing Chakra Meditation. You can also use the aid of crystals to assist in the cycle of healing, revitalizing, when doing Chakra Meditation. Chakra Meditation can be a powerful healing meditation and harmful emotion clearing.

Vipassana - Vipassana Meditation is the fourth meditation method. Vipassana Meditation is one of the most ancient types of meditation, and is used to gain insight into one's existence and the nature of reality. The aim of Vipassana Meditation is to bring an end to the individual's suffering. This is done by adding the three factors that are impermanence, pain and not-self. After a long period of practice in Vipassana Meditation, the meditator will come to a point where they distinguish these three requirements from themselves and attain nirvana. Both physical and psychological problems are assumed not to be part of the true self or the "I," and should be removed with the practice of Vipassana Meditation.

Raja - The last mediation strategy we'll be learning about is meditation on Raja. Through Raja Meditation the subconscious is called supreme, and taming the feelings and the body is the duty of the minds. Raja Meditation tries to get the subconscious to take full control of the body and feelings. Raja Meditation and associated activities are a form of meditation which is very systematic. We are expected to give up stuff like sex, alcohol, meat and pay close attention to their acts when a person takes up Raja Meditation. The reason for giving up these things in Raja Meditation is that it trains the body and mind to meditate.

Above is a quick line out of five common methods for meditation. I hope this little essay has given you enough details to lead you in the direction of the meditation technique you want to explore more.

If you are taking up a certain meditation technique, it is recommended that you adopt a good detailed curriculum.

What Techniques are right for me in meditation?

What's therapy, exactly? You ask people, and they will most likely refer you to "Wikipedia" on the internet. On the internet you can find thousands of web pages which describe the meditation exercise and attempt to explain it in their own words. Unfortunately, many of these places describe meditation in a very complex and abstract way... Incredibly hard to understand and just plain boring.

The site that describes meditation very explicitly so far, is Wikipedia. Possibly an activity or practice that enhances your consciousness is one of the best ways to describe this workout.

In particular, meditative techniques help you to attain a self-awareness. It does so as meditation techniques focus the mind to push through the noise of emotions and jumbled patterns of thinking. The goal is to be able to think more easily and get more confident. Therefore all these techniques allow us to do this.

Life's pressures can have a dramatic effect upon us. When we try to tackle all the various problems that come our way, we get emotionally worn down. Much the same way our bodies need proper exercise to stay healthy, so our brains need proper relaxation in order to remain successful. We do this by getting better attuned to our consciousness. Practicing meditation techniques is actually the only way to achieve this task on a permanent basis. When you meditate correctly, you are liberating the mind from burdensome, noisy patterns of thought. Who wouldn't want less tension and more focus? Sure, so these strategies can essentially allow you to become more confident, think clearly, concentrate better and more. But these things are not the act of contemplation, in and of themselves. It is not sleep to focus on something. It is not either to place the self in a comfortable role or to do other poses. There are a variety of meditation techniques that will help a person throughout their life achieve plenty of benefits.

Popular Meditation Techniques

1. Zen-Zen Meditation is one of the most common and well-known meditative techniques. This method of contemplation had been developed by Zen monks. Zen is about reaching an absolute state of stillness and silence. Although Zen meditative methods are known to be among the simplest and most effective to execute, it takes time and effort to learn them. This approach is based on sitting in the place of the lotus in order to achieve a calm meditation.

2. Mantra-The Mantra is another well-known mediation method. Mantra is an activity in their minds that many people tend to associate with meditation. Mantra techniques include chanting or' mantra repetition.' This is a technique of meditation which achieves a state of awareness by using the music. Yes, one of America's most common methods-transindental meditation-is an example of a mantra meditation.

3. Vipassana-Vipassana is a third well known technique. Vipassana is a breathing-focusing, Buddhist practice. When we consider the fact that breathing is an activity of every moment and a need to survive, then we can begin to see how it can have significance to focus on this aspect of life. Vipassana is a method of meditation that basically allows one to be mindful of their breathing, from which (when done properly) a state of consciousness is attained.

Many Techniques Several many techniques are available. Such three also happen to be the west's most well recognized and studied. What you'll find is that all three have the same goal in mind-that is to achieve a higher consciousness level. Note, one of the most important meditative aims is to become more mindful of the self, which in effect creates a healthy mind. It's fascinating that the aim stays the same irrespective of the variations between the meditation techniques.

All the variations in the strategies mentioned in this book are in turn indicators of how each contributes to the same goal— that of awareness-raising. It's like the saying goes "all roads lead to Rome." In this situation, in addition to many other kinds of mental, spiritual, financial, and physical rewards all these different techniques contribute to enlightenment and knowledge.

Whether the calming method you use is based on sitting, driving, laying down, listening, saying a phrase, or singing, it will bring benefits to your everyday life and benefits to those around you throughout their lives.

The Most Effective Meditation Method for Opening The Third Eye Chakra

It is said that the third eye is the source of greater intelligence and psychic powers. This offers one the opportunity to experience telepathy, astral journeys and past lives.

Third-eye meditations revolve around the sixth chakra, or what is also known as the "Agya Chakra" between the eyes, which is said to be the "third-eye" region.

There are several third-eye opening methods for meditation, but one of the most effective is a very easy one to introduce.

Here are the steps you will take: a. Open eyes b. Slow down the intake, a sweet, steadily steady rhythm c. Pull the chin down, as if dragged by its weight d. Only keep breathing steadily before you feel pretty comfortable. When you close your eyes, look up at your third eye region with your inner eyes. Only focus your attention on that region and you'll see that you're' looking up' without even opening your eyes. Keep breathing steady and peaceful g. Relax the eyes as they are locked, and gaze upwards. Attempt not to' look up' the feet, keep them comfortable h. Keep at it for a few minutes at a time Integrate this form of meditation into your daily practice, ideally every day during the same period and in the same place, so that your body and mind embrace the position as your regular place of meditation. This will bring you into a state of meditation quicker than you would otherwise. Your third eye chakra will expand with practice, and slowly, little by little, you may find little stuff you may not have seen before, your awareness of information, and your' six-sense' will improve.

This method of meditation will help you calm your mind from a full, stressful day, and will encourage you to draw inner strength from your own.

Meditation benefits

- Greater clarity of mind
- More relaxed states of mind
- Greater capacity to focus
- Greater imagination and insight

If you're new to meditation, the mind runs around with thoughts like: "What should I do? Is this all there is to it? What should I feel?" The downside of meditating at the same time each day is that your biorhythms, like waking, eating and falling asleep, would automatically respond to it as routine. At a given time, the nervous system will become used to meditation, enabling you to reach deep meditative states more quickly.

Make sure you turn your cell off. If you have teenagers, set aside a period when they are in or sleeping at night.

Build Your Room Develop a wall between you and the outer environment even if you're just meditating for ten minutes.

The Strategy of Meditation

Where to Meditate? Book a special place to meditate in your house. If you have the house, it can be as easy as putting a comfortable chair or pillow aside, or an entire room. Put a lamp, roses, or any special items that are of spiritual significance to you on an altar table. Creating a space designated for contemplation benefits as Divine Forces collect in the position where you meditate; making it easier to stay in the same place every time you sit. Like heading to a temple, church or place of worship, all you need to do with regular practice is sit in that position to feel comfortable, calm and relaxed.

It can take many months of meditation during your meditation practice to regularly achieve theta levels. Sacred Ground lets you achieve certain thresholds faster, so you can start experiencing the life-changing effects. Whether you are, or are seasoned, a novice meditator, let Sacred Ground carry you to your inner world.

Build a Reverent Atmosphere. Invent your own practice of sootiness before meditation. Perhaps it's after a bath in the dark, or at sunrise before the rest of the world is up. Light a candle, take a few deep breaths and dedicate your practice to revealing the highest potential you have. Should you like, say a prayer, chant or light any incense. A calm, reverent environment can trigger a state of contemplation. Many people find music to be effective in meditation.

Line yourself for meditation. Sit up straight with your back. When appropriate, carry pillows behind your back for protection. Getting your spine straight is vital because energy can travel freely up and down your spine. You should sit flat on the floor with your feet cross-legged or on a comfortable chair. You can also lie down, placing the hands under a cushion. While meditating, whenever you tend to fall asleep, it's best to sit up so you can stay awake.

Tip: Theta is meditation strength. Since theta is right on the edge of the delta, synonymous with sleep, slipping into a nap instead of meditation is normal for beginning meditators. If you easily fall asleep while you meditate consider using Brain Power. This harmoniously stacks theta waves to keep you awake and safe, with very high beta frequencies.

How long will I meditate? It depends on you how much you meditate every day. A good start is ten to fifteen minutes a day. You may notice that, by inserting five minutes here and there, you simply extend your mediation period. Another approach to increase the period you spend meditating is to set a goal of adding five minutes each week until you follow a twenty to thirty minute natural rhythm. To be overly ambitious is one of the drawbacks of starting meditators. Trust your intuition, and continue with a time that's relaxed for you.

Registered meditators typically spend an hour of contemplation per day. If you can work up to 40 to 60 minutes slowly the greater the success will be. Consistency offers significant long-term benefits.

The key is getting things completed every day. The Therapy results are cumulative. Richard Davidson, a psychology and psychiatry professor at the University of Wisconsin, states, "Modern neuroscience demonstrates that our brains are as fluid as our bodies. Meditation can help you strengthen the mind in the same manner as meditation will improve the body." Thus, any minute you meditate, you enhance the brain's biochemistry, build muscles that increase your concentration, and so on.

Relax, breathe and relax, take long, steady, deep breaths while you meditate. Give the oxygen deep into your belly and exhale. Every time you breathe in picture your body being flooded with healing electricity. Ask your body to let go of pain and stress as you breathe out.

Tip: Each exhalation counts to calm a busy mind, beginning with one going up to ten, then start the cycle all over again. When you forget where you are, move back to one and continue all over again. Do this, to slow down mental activity for ten minutes. Lots of ideas will come and go in the beginning. If you realize that you are distracted, switch your mind to your air. Linger on the quiet area in your feelings. The room is expected to grow in time.

Relax with a Body Scan. A body scan calms the nervous system, reduces anxiety and allows you to feel represented-sometimes we spend so much time in our minds that we forget we have a body.

It is a workout in itself to perform this activity for five to ten minutes. Once you meditate, it is also a great way to settle down.

To continue with, guide your mind to explore your left foot. Note the physical sensations around the foot and within. Instead transfer your consciousness up your left leg, arm, thigh and right hip. Imagine having to travel through the lungs, muscles and bones. You can consider energy blocks or numbness places. You can sense the waves tingling, as the cells come alive from your active attention. Only follow the sensations. Experiment with how to say the muscles to relax and actually let go by focusing the power.

Do the same with your right foot, with your right hip leg up. Guide your mind to the region around the root chakra-the belly and the buttocks. Next explore your hands, stomach and arms, moving to your mouth. Then shift to your left hand, experience the vibrations in each of your fingertips, then fly to your left shoulder up your neck. Repeat right-handedly.

Explore your chest and neck; see how you can relax, and stretch your stomach. Move into your head, and calm your face and neck. Enable softening and relaxation of the muscles across the neck, temples and forehead.

Tip: EEG (electroencephalogram) research has revealed that theta stimulation travels more quickly into the frontal cortex when the eyes, temples and scalp are comfortable. When you relax those muscles you can go further into a meditative state.

How to communicate with the subconscious? Improve the benefits of meditation even if you are a novice meditator. Balance the chakras, become optimistic and reduce anxiety; improve your immune system and grow imagination, just by listening to Deep Meditation.

The first aim in meditation is to note random thoughts and to keep quiet. Throughout his book Learn to Meditate, David Fontana, Ph.D. advises, "Watching your emotions and trying to recognise them as triggers you have begun the journey to meditation." As you practice meditation you will become conscious of how the mind loops throughout motion with many separate thoughts and memories.

The mind will be like a chatterbox at first, moving from one problem to another, that is normal. You may be stuck worrying about the job or solving problems. You may be concerned about something that hasn't changed yet or remembering stuff you've missed, like paying your credit card bill.

Mark Your Thinking. Observe and then mark the consistency of your thinking. "These are stressful, job feelings," "those thoughts are pessimistic and restricting," or "Here we go with my To Do list again." So softly shift your mind to your breath and move into the gap between your emotions.

Each time you recognize the consistency of your feelings, you take huge measures in contemplation which will eventually occur in your life. In time you are going to become a keen observer of your inner world. When you have slipped into negative thinking you will note and strive to turn your mind to feelings that broaden and strengthen your sense of self.

The highest possible level of thinking is optimistic. Positive thoughts soothe the nervous system and encourage sense of well-being and wholeness.

When negative emotions, such as rage, guilt, anxiety or sorrow, emerge, mark them and then turn your attention gently to something good.

Meditate Upon Your Divine Self. A beneficial activity is to meditate on your divine self, the self which contains vast potential and gifts. Use your imagination to explore the magnificent being within you. Drink from the well of wisdom that multiplies the happiness and fulfillment in life. The practice is about discovering and communicating the divine nature. Directed meditations that will help you create uplifting states of being and reach your higher self: Guided Meditation, Reclaim Your Destiny, Satisfy Your Heart's Desire, Live Prayer.

Finish with a Feeling. Just settle down for a moment at the end of your meditation session, feeling the energy flowing inside the body. Before you jump back into the world this delay helps you to incorporate the meditation session into your daily life.

Guided Chakra Meditations Using Reiki

This therapy technique is ideal for any degree learning Reiki. You will adapt this technique to match your own style as you become more acquainted with the chakra method. Sit in relation to the lotus. Close your eyes, and track the wind through your nose. This practice is a strong way to examine the chakra awareness when transmitting energy to relevant issues. The following example relates to the chakra center. Depend on just one chakra for all of your practice, which can last from 20 to 30 minutes. Keep meditating on the corresponding chakra every day. For specific information about each chakra please refer to my other posts on this website. Speak softly and clearly to yourself, maintaining a good attentiveness throughout the session. A template, although random, may follow these lines: place your hands on your root chakra and ask Reiki to work. Remain silent between each phrase for the length of 3 to 4 breaths Imagine red light curing your root The root chakra grows during the first year of existence; help cure any problems from that time in my life. Second, be mindful that any shortcomings or limitations must be recognized as a real aspect of your existence.

This does not mean that you have to spend your entire life with those vulnerabilities. If you have grown from these struggles successfully and make a conscious decision to remove them, then you are really primed for recovery and change. Reflect on each chakra for 5 minutes in the accompanying exercise to strengthen the healing process. This takes about 35 minutes for a full meditation on all 7 chakras.

Make positive comments for each chakra Inhale deeply and relieve discomfort with each exhale Position your hands on your root chakra, feel your life force and sense of belonging to the universe; feel some love and security issues; confirm that the world loves me and fulfills my needs; let the Reiki flow to your navel (sacred) chakra; believe that your body is well balanced; affirm I de' Such Reiki meditations can be alternated with self-healing exercises, or quiet reflection. Determine each day what exercise would best serve your well-being.

Seven Components of Chakra Meditation

Perhaps you think of meditation as an act of sitting with your legs crossed and humming yourself. Okay, not all of this is about contemplation.
You can find several different forms of meditation which will help you relax and reduce stress. Chakra is a special form of meditation that originates from Hindu beliefs. Today the practice of contemplation on chakras has spread to every corner of the globe.

Chakra means the corporeal source of spiritual power. It is focused on seven separate parts of the self and each component has its own specific colour, feature, and body region. When a difference exists in any of the seven different parts, it breaks the understanding of the inner self as a whole.

Each chakra is connected with various problems, and many meditation techniques include solutions to solve them.
Muladhara: Red / Earth This chakra is located at the root of the spinal cord. The most important chakra is known to be this. It may well be linked to the survival instincts and physical integrity of one's own. This chakra can be used to get you health and safety.
Svadhisthana: Orange / Water The core of the emotional and sexual impulses resides here. This chakra is in the lower back and belly, taking us close to each other. Focusing on this chakra will improve the emotional control, sexual satisfaction and changeability.
Anahata: Green / Air Anahata holds peace and love within you. It has to do with the heart and opposites such as male and female, and with the mind and body. It also takes you to an acceptable state of mind.
Manipura: Yellow / Fire This chakra is about your relationship with the ego. It also refers to the force of your will. It is responsible for digestion in the body. By meditating on this chakra you'll get power and energy.
Vishuddha: Blue / Signal This chakra is the imagination core. This helps you show yourself. This reflects the waves, cultures, and smells, as it is situated in the mouth.
Ajna: Yellow / White Ajna helps people think more clearly and see better. Sometimes recognized as the 3rd eye. This allows for illumination and reflection. It makes you feel mentally and physically healthier.
Sahasrara: Violet / Thinking Although it is not considered superior to other chakras, it is the only deeply connected chakra with the universe outside. This chakra brings you peace, faith and mysterious knowledge. It is linked to self-awareness and perception. It is considered the corporeal cap.
The secret to meditating on chakras lies in knowing all the chakras and what they signify. Once all the chakras are aligned, you'll reach the level of Sahasrara, which will give you a deeper understanding of life. That will create peace and happiness for you. You will try to develop control upon each of them after practicing all seven sections of this meditation.
End Note! After practicing chakra meditation you will realize how each of these seven chakras is linked to your condition in your life. This will help you focus on that particular branch until the total disparity is rectified. Continuous analysis of this practice will bring you a state of peace and joy within.

Rewards of Chakra Meditation in Yoga Class

As mystical force flows upward through the seven main chakras, in a process known as a kundalini awakening, the body opens to spiritual awareness. Beginners are recommended to undergo formal instruction until they carry this lesson anywhere. This method of mediation may be performed by seasoned practitioners or guided by a qualified teacher of Yoga.

The Seven Main Chakras: Each chakra is correlated with emotional and physical conditions associated with that particular body region. There is also a colour and a musical note linked to each and these are often used in meditations on chakras.

1. Node-Root 2. Spleen or Sacral-orange 3. Plexus Solar-yellow 4. Coeur-green 5. Throat-White 6. Third Eye-Native 7. Crown-violet chakra meditation Chakra meditation is much like any other meditation, but emphasis is put on each chakra separately, beginning with the root and progressing upward. Three to four minutes are usually spent on each, but the mediation practitioner may intuitively know that one or more chakras take longer. For more efficient outcomes the whole cycle can also be replicated. Although not required, guided and musical meditations are especially effective in visualizing energy that moves through the chakra.

The Chakras store thoughts and emotions. We need to be published to avoid blockages and health-related complications. Not only does chakra meditation unload old feelings and habits of thought, it also makes room for new development and imagination. Specific benefits linked to managing each chakra are:• Core-physical security• Sacral-emotions, attraction, imagination • Solar Plexus-center of personal power • Heart-feelings of love and caring• Throat-communication, self-expression • 3rd Eye-intuition, inspiration, spirituality • Crown-unity with the cosmos While each chakra has its own nature, everything functions t Energy rises from the foundation and passes upward but can only pass across clear and strong chakras. Chakra mediation is one of the most effective ways of expanding the flow of awareness and achieving emotional, physical, and spirit peace.

Techniques To Do Chakras Meditation Effectively

Chakra Meditations are a powerful technique that can benefit you in many respects. The chakras are the core of your body, seven go from the base of your spine to the head crown. We reflect various aspects of your mind, body and soul. Growing regulates some part of the body, but also some facets of the spirit. Such chakras are depicted in light spokes, each with a specific rainbow hue. They can also be used to help alleviate other common illnesses, just to name a handful, including heart disease, stomach problems, and even mental health. If you are involved in this strong practice, here are seven tips to help you get the most out of your meditation experience.

The first suggestion is to become fully acquainted with chakras. Which means what it is, what it does and how it affects your life. There are seven, each doing specific things and being linked to various parts of your body. For help you achieve self-healing, restoring yourself, or helping you strive for deeper awakening levels, then you need to learn what each signifies. Online, you will find an array of different chakra based tools.

The second tip is that if you really take this exercise seriously, you need to set aside time, as well as a dedicated place to meditate. You must also customize your area with things related to this meditation. For starters, a broad chakra map is used by many people to help them concentrate on a specific chakra. Perhaps using colored candles, or carrying stones or fabric, or illumination to help you imagine the different chakras in your head.

The third approach is performing your own meditations. People have difficulty accepting new concepts, as always. While the notion of a chakra is not old, the term isn't common to many citizens in the Western World. The biggest problems encountered by those who want to do this form of therapy is family and friends mockery. Repeat before they question you how you always get so centered, in good health, and so on, before asking them what you're doing.

Holding in this practice is another really good tip. You can notice that your chakras are totally out of sync so they will not be realigned by one or two sessions.

Nevertheless, once you've got them back in line, you've got to have daily internal' maintenance' to keep them that way. Which takes a lifetime commitment if you are really concerned.

When meditating on these chakras it is important that you keep your focus on the target. Either to help heal other parts of your body, or to align your chakras, you should always have a reason. When you begin to see progress, don't get overly excited, as that will bring a shock on your body. On the other side, the chakras may be so whacked out that it needs a dozen sessions to begin to feel the benefits.

Still make good use of the chakras. You want to do this exercise to make your life better, not making yourself stronger than everybody else. If people start seeing the change in your personality, your overall life attitude, or your ailments tend to go down, don't get a big head on it. This alone will start putting them out of sync.

Though this is the seventh tip, it may also be the most significant tip. Chakras are a powerful tool but it may take time to bring these chakras back into alignment so that you can see results from your efforts.

This didn't happen over night that your chakras were all out of whack. Everyone is special and each has its own problems. Another individual can immediately feel the effects whilst it can take weeks or months for others. Don't be frustrated and stay tuned. At the end of the rainbow Chakra is a glow. It will become simpler as you get better at doing these chakra meditations, and you will realize that you learn more about yourself, your faith, and that you can do all the stuff you want to do in your life, and that impact can extend to all those around you.

Chapter 8: Activating the Third Eye through body purification

Have you ever been to a numerologist? If you have one of the following questions you might have asked yourself: how can this person know so much about me? How could the forecasts be so right? Is that man a magician? The fact is that a correct reading of numerology rests only on an accessible chakra of the third eye.

-number brings, according to various scholars, specific laws and energies which are implied by the date of birth of each individual. Like each person, these numbers have different characteristics and results which can help you determine your performance, income, mood, power and any other attribute. The main question, though, is - how can a person find out about his or her correct numbers and their results? Until we start digging for answers, let's determine that a healthy third-eye chakra is required in order to continue. Numerology talent isn't very hard to attain. All you need to do is open your intuitive chakra and just like a numerologist, you will predict your potential.
You can see things of perceptible scope with an active third-eye chakra. Nevertheless, staying balanced and loading yourself back up with love and light when you're through is always a good thing. Opening the third eye chakra is an agonizing operation that can sometimes exhaust you absolutely. It helps you see clearly, get a deeper understanding and view things in detail.
Through trade I am a qualified numerologist. I always wanted to experience the advantages of numerology. And as it happens, the feeling of happiness and the enlightening awareness I gained by expanding my mind helped me dig more. I consider soothing chakras.
I'm really impressed with my latest perceptive abilities. It helps me to see things more clearly, and to know what is right and wrong, obviously. It's like an internal map working inside of me; it's a hand guiding me in the direction of what to do. I realize what I want to do and I am aware of the consequences of my actions. I'd never have it any other way.

"To be conscious is to be responsible." Even though opening the third eye chakra may seem to make you feel like holding the world on your hands, it's actually the exact opposite of that. It is completely empowering. I realize what I need to do now, and how to do it.

Now I am willing to use my numerological abilities to support those around me. My third-eye chakra healing has given me enormous powers and a dynamic personality. My contributions were compensated for and I had found my love for numerology. From top business tycoons to royal families, powerful politicians, curing physicians, movie stars, professional athletes and the ordinary person, my healthy chakra has helped me to help these people accomplish what they want: a sense of balance in their lives.

Whenever someone asks me if they should seek chakra healing or how the third eye chakra can benefit them, my response is: "I'm not asking you to change your life, I'm telling you to enjoy it with everything you want." That's how chakra balancing supported me and that's how it helps you.

Unblock Your Third Eye Chakra Utilizing Brainwave Entrainment

Brainwave Entrainment, a technically developed device that can change your brainwaves to pulse at a frequency that can unblock your Third Eye Chakra.

Repeated and rhythmic sound waves are inserted into your brain, with the goal of modifying the level of your primary brainwave. Because of a rule of psychology, the frequency following the law of reaction, the brain must naturally follow and mimic the stimulation, and lead you easily to the frequency that will unblock your Third Eye Chakra.

The Chakra of the Third Eye is about redemption and mercy and symbolizes a condition of liberation or the evocation of mental images which have a deep connection to your divine source.

This Chakra is directly related to your source.

The Chakra in the Third Eye is aligned with...

- Experiences with perception, clairvoyance, precognition and out-of-body.
- Capable of seeing auras.
- To be the seer.
- Intuition.
- Male and feminine forces combine.
- Brain and pituitary gland.
- Brain health, skin, nose and sinuses, facial and neural system.
- Indigo children born with a fully open Third Eye.

- In the corner of your eye you can see non-visible objects because your actual eyesight can overlap your inner vision.
- You will witness telepathy, astral projection and past lives at this location.

Era of Growth

- With your Third Eye open you are born and you can see certain dimensions quickly. That's why it's common for kids to have invisible friends they can see and nobody else can imagine.

- As you get older, that skill is lost, because you are affected by the older generation who believe that everything is in the mind.

Can be triggered during teenagers, get bursts from it (most at this stage don't open the door, but some do), but it's more popular between the ages of 36 and 42. Whatever occurs over this period of time can impact your third eye protection.
- You will have a damaged chakra when there was pain during this period.

A Safe Way, Unblocked Third Eye Chakra

- You are willing to see yourself as a visually trained divine being.
- Using your creativity, and innate intuition, you build your own truth.

High mental ability.

- Reason and feeling mix.
- Well generally safe, clear thinking and centered... Clear, nimble thinking.
- Make a large amount of work in a short time.
- You don't have a lot of thoughts and fears based on mental chatter-fear to confuse your instincts and expectations.
- You have a good memory and the presentation is perfect.
- Something you can envision and have appear in the real.

- You have the opportunity to see what's covered up.
- You acquire clear-sighted powers, most usually telepathy. We also share the natural ability. Telepathy is the mutual inconscious receipt of signals and emotions.

Unblocking your Third Eye Chakra through brainwave trainings is a quick and easy way to reach the most powerful and highest source of ethereal energy available to you in your human form, enabling you to explore different realms without having to leave your body by telepathy, astral travel and past lives.

Clearing each of your chakras and managing them will allow you to live your best life. Profit from a brainwave entrainment system, which can easily access and sustain the frequency needed to trigger the chakras.

Seeing Outside Visible Existence Through Brainwave Entraining

The most strong and ultimate source of etheric energy available to you in your human form falls through your Third Eye Chakra, rendering it one of the most essential Chakras. Brainwave entrainment is a tool that, through the Third Eye Chakra, will enable you experience different aspects without having to leave the body.

Entraining introduces to the brain a rhythmic and repetitive auditory stimulation that it will imitate and emulate, modifying the strength of its brainwave to suit opening and activating the Third Eye Chakra.

Developing this Chakra, utilizing brainwave trainings in this lifetime, would enable you to use your instincts during your decision-making process, rather than simply relying on your physical senses.

When the Chakra in the Third Eye is open...

- It is directly related to your origins, or to the divine.
- Is a source of personal understanding of your perceptions.
- Gives you the ability to distinguish truth from illusion, helping you to go beyond narrow thought, use logical, analytical logic.
- Frustration, hatred and resentment, breakup of the self, circumstances, prejudices, behaviors and perceptions are all let go.
- It's the place where you sense isolation.
- Is the small gate that paves the way for your consciousness to climb the Crown Chakra.
- This is the location from which all dreams derive.

- The Third Eye is where you free from poor expectations bad programming, so you can discover your own unique intelligence. Your spiritual abilities grow as you do this.
- Seeing the possibilities. For second sight the Third Eye Chakra is responsible.
- You have the ability to receive non-verbal signals through this chakra, even from the past or the future and definitely from the current.
- Communications are not restricted to space or time, or scope.
- You can see ghosts, demons, and things that are not apparent.
- Sometimes, you can see the history.
- You understand the strength is in here and now.
- The Karma is transcended when released.
- The visions you have when unblocked are positive, spiritual.

Spiritual Lesson of the Third Eye Chakra

- Comprehending what is true and what is imagination, how to disconnect and open your mind.
- Realisation of the spirit, intuition, creativity, clear-sightedness, focus and peace of mind.
- Intelligence, commitment and understanding outside our earthly world's duality;
- Trust the wisdom and experience which comes from your soul's perspective.
- Looking beyond the boundaries of everyday life.
- Knowledge of the passions.
- Do not use the actual eyes to "see."

Using brainwave entrainment to unlock the Third Eye

Chakra enhances your mental abilities, deepens your ability to concentrate and lets you reach your inner knowledge.
You're developing the capacity to see what's secret.
This is a great way to get your life off track.
Clearing each of your chakras and managing them will allow you to live your best life.
Benefit from a brainwave entrainment system, which can easily access and sustain the frequency needed to trigger the chakras.

Chapter 9: How to Protect Yourself during Third Eye Activation

How can you be safe and healthy with your Chakras?

You're going to sense it!
Spiritually...you're going to feel a higher mental pulse... You are going to have a new understanding of the question which caused emotional imbalances... Physically, you might feel the necessity to release, followed by intense euphoria... In one day or two, you may feel ill because your body is washing itself and then feeling good.

Healing Third Eye Chakra on Animals

Working with animals and healing is such a rewarding experience not only for the animal with the physical, mental, emotional or spiritual issue but also for the healing practitioner. They can use a variety of animal treatment methods, such as energy work, vibrational, use of stones, relaxation, acupuncture, acupressure, and much more.
Find out what works best and what area you're drawn to before you start your pet healing session.
On an object the sixth chakra is identical to the one of a human. This region of the chakra is called the third eye or brow chakra, is located in the middle of the forehead just above the eyes and is synonymous with purple and violet colour. Now there is some controversy around the colorations of the sixth and seventh chakras with the inclusion for these chakras of indigo, red, violet, and black or white colours. Either the purple / violet hue can be correlated with the sixth chakra and it can also be aligned with indigo shading. For your work with humans and animals alike, please feel free to use what resonates inside you.

Chapter 10: Various Factors That Could Influence The Awakening

Awakening the Third Eye Through Quantum Consciousness - How Humanity Awakens

Before this can occur there is much more moving[of illusory conviction to perceptions — which are backed by our imagined visions and some imagination, and then to spiritual inner knowledge] that must arise in all minds.
Total reawakening, in other words, will end the illusion of separation.
Since your body is not the true you, I use the term "mate" to convey solidarity and harmony beyond any body gender connotations that would only bring duality of thinking to the image. In this harmony is where we learn to trust our true inner voice that guides us to the life we really want to live My own internal place through quantum consciousness is one step behind many, and one step ahead of many others, in a continuous line of peace procession.
This stream of reality is the interlocking chain of oneness that is called the cycle of waking mankind.
This includes undoing errors in our thinking with corrections which lead to total harmony of mind.
When expectations fade away causing awareness to change deeper and become mere information, the mind of humanity must regenerate, and in every moment the process is going on, everywhere,. The transition I'm thinking about where society is evolving is a simple move from wrong-mindedness to right-mindedness, and from there to awareness bridge over.
So long as there is time there will be some ego-based holes in its line, or broken ties. Nevertheless, there will be a point in time when the spaces before us and behind us will be filled, and the chain of God's One-Mind will be completely bound and eternally welded together. The transformation internally focuses upon the outer world.
There is a new way of perceiving the world going on all over, as the light of truth becomes stronger with the use of time by the Holy Spirit. This is how true knowledge grows in us all.

Regardless of your level of involvement as mankind awakens on this path, you are together with me and all the others as an example of the wholeness of feeling, one with Christ, one with His Father, or the whole Child of God. When we pause to get hung up on a conventional term, we can praise ego based intrusion.

When mankind awakens it will show that time and space never really existed. Waking up involves absolutely undoing thinking mistakes, and becoming new.

There was a moment where, if someone wakes up to me with a tale about life or universal awareness, I'd think they'd be nuts. The portion of your mind that wants to know more is the true you, and you have been invited as a brother / sister to awaken the detailed third eye of quantum consciousness.

Let me say I know just how many of you need to sound.

To you woman reading along, please don't be offended when I talk to you as a brother when I say brother / sister, or speak of the "father" of Christ, or refer to God as "He." These are just traditional short hands to you— for the Union.

It's the sense behind the term we're searching for, because we express brotherhood as the whole Child of God, and as One Mind— the mind behind the flesh.

Ego preservation continues No question when you learn about mankind emerging, or quantum consciousness— waking the third eye, some of you may want to laugh in disbelief; but I think another part of you will want to know more as well.

This last part of you is the same aspect of me that keeps writing about my observations of never-ending patient recovery and development spurts. The intentional recovery and development happens in spurts because of ego intervention that tries to obstruct it.

Foods That Help Balance The Third Eye Chakra

The chakras are the source of your strength. They are places in your body that store your latent energies. These are openings for the force of energy to flood into and out of the sensations. We show your self-awareness and we cultivate your spirit. If in that situation they are published it's like fuel for your soul. We are close to a power pipe, with divine illumination at its top.

If your chakras are accessible, you will equate the blossom of a lotus to your life. While a lotus blossom blooms beautifully in water, when your chakras are excited, so does your life. Third eye chakra is a power source for vision and instinctive beliefs.

For anyone, making choices is important and you should make sure that he has this skill and use it effectively as well. If you face different setbacks with your ability to make choices in that case it has been strongly suggested that you should be extremely aware of the third-eye chakra. In such a situation, the removal of the third eye chakra will be necessary in order to restore everything to the normal standard which can be deemed useful. With the opening of the third eye chakra, the relaxation techniques are calculated to be incredibly significant, since you can definitely obtain excellent benefits with it. If you're worried about your life and are eager to get better results with good choices in that case you should invent different methods of massage for opening the third eye chakra. The sixth chakra is engaged in both the perception and skill creation, and the recognition that what you see has an influence on you. While your two eyes perceive earth as material, your sixth chakra perceives it past the physical. This picture is telepathy, clear-sightedness, vision, insight, creativity, and imagining. In the Third Eye Chakra too much stress will contribute to headaches, concentrating problems, anxiety and hallucinations. A weak sixth chakra will cause poor vision and memory problems. Grape juice and red wine are the most common and useful foods for balancing the third-eye chakra, so if someone wants to balance his or her third chakra then try to eat those foods regularly and timely.

If you are eager to ensure that you embrace an incredibly excellent life, one of the most vital features in this case is the harmonization of your third-eye chakra. Similar to your body, which needs nourishment, vitamins and proteins to keep going, your chakras also need food to be well-nourished and balanced and to be ready. The items you can include for calming and nourishing the Third Eye Chakra are: herbs and dark blue fruits, such as blackberries, blueberries and aubergines, can help to rouse the Third Eye Chakra. Apart from poppy seed and lavender perfume, grape juice and red wine can also serve to rouse the mental core.

Your Third Eye Chakra & Your Health - Intuition, Awareness & Headaches

We are all born with two eyes and although our degrees of sight can vary from person to person, we can still say yes, we have two eyes and we can see "this" well.
So how much more do you suppose you'd do if you'd got a third eye?
Which could alter you think? Would you have better vision? Less Evidently? Can you picture this third eye granting yourself some sort of super-human vision or skill?
The good news is you were always born with a third eye. The extra eye takes the form of Ajna, the sixth chakra or source of strength. Your Third Eye is conveniently situated under and just above your eyes, and is called the seat of insight and home to your intellect and creativity.

And in addition, by getting this extra eye, you are actually given a very rare, almost super-human skill and that is the gift of intuition-the position where you can link your mental and spiritual abilities.
(Minus the references to the crystal ball, of course.) Your intuition is properly called your sixth sense-after sight, smell, taste, touch and hearing, your five senses-and also because it is closely involved in your sixth chakra. There are amazing links that are already recognized in our everyday lives when it comes to chakra system wisdom-the first step is always understanding of it.
Awareness is the Third Eye chakra's second bestowal.
We are granted knowledge as a means to see things more clearly, to see circumstances more thoroughly and, from that point of view, to be able to make deliberate and correct decisions.
But these talents sound like a lot of pressure can be upon them.
Living by insight and perception always seems like you're signing up for a holier life than you do.

And because of that, this chakra's dysfunction will manifest as a second guess, nervousness, flightiness, anxiety, pupils, mouth, nose and sinus infections, hormonal imbalances, insomnia and anxious disorders. Depression can also result from an imbalanced Chakra of the Third Eye.
Another interesting side effect of the mismatch might be a frustration with the status quo or deflation, especially in your life career field.
It's almost as if the body knows you're not quite in contact with your instincts, or your mind isn't where it could be, and that's why it turns out to be an undercurrent and almost deceptive discomfort or unhappiness.
Many diseases with the headaches, skin, mouth, nose, or sinus take a little time to cure.
This may be directly related to the gradual disintegration of what's going within the brain.
Look around and see what is going on in your life, really see.
Where do you feel happy? Where do you disappoint?
Are you having trouble focusing? Do you feel nervous, uncertain or flighty?
Would you feel disconnected with the day-to-day things you are doing? In what ways, if so?
Can you see how all of this relates directly to our health?
Experiencing the fever, experiencing the sinus infection or feeling detached to your surroundings is not enough; you also need to act on it.
Imagine that, equilibrium here implies clear thinking, a good sense of direction and commitment, a deep creativity, a strong sense of self-realization and a healthy nervous and endocrine system.
If something is off here then it sounds to the whole body.

The Third Eye chakra can almost seem like the brain's nerve center, which, well, it really is. So how do we deal with imbalances here? How can we translate these ideas into greater health?

There are a few really easy ideas I have for the Third Eye, many of which demand that you be alone with your feelings and alone. When you find it incredibly challenging to do that, then I'll give you a solution for that too.

Yoga and meditation are the choices for fast monitoring towards a more relaxed Third Eye chakra. That doesn't mean the procedure is either fast or painless, however. Both will pose several problems, past and present, and need to be treated with that in mind.

Journalising your thoughts is another choice, especially if you find it difficult to keep your mind quiet. It is also useful for working through any of the issues brought up by yoga or meditation.

If you find it difficult to be alone with your reflections, may I recommend a guided meditation or a manual for you. Because you are asked to do something or visualize it, the brain will come out of defense, defensive mode and be responsive to slowing down and relaxing.

Its nervous system is the key here. If your body gets put on the alert, it's going to intensify the nervous system and find it impossible to get out of the emergency mode. But if you can find a way to calm the mind, slow down the nervous system and return to homeostasis, then you will notice that this chakra allows wellbeing as easy as relaxing.

Chapter 11: How To Maintain The Energies

It is my belief that everyone can teach themselves to sense and control their energy system successfully-things such as seeing the light, performing divination, metaphysical and remote healing, and psychological defense against aggressive energy forces, given they understand the principles behind the energy system and how to build and handle it. There is no mystery surrounding this inherent talent with which we are to be born but have overlooked and missed it through the passage of time. For the Higher Spirits have decided to hide within us the secret of life and give us the ability to rediscover it and bring it to our own good use. It is our utter arrogance and ignorance that would always prevent us from enjoying this gift of life. It is by increasing our energy awareness that we learn the ability to manage it, and the more we are on the path to achieving harmony of Light, the more we focus on it. To real psychics, those who only travel high in the presence of their strong guides are not usually those who are weak and defenseless when the guides are no longer there to shield them and render their offers.

Chakras And Power Hidden in Body

We need to learn that not only do we have a physical body but we also have a power body, or a set of hidden energy body more accurately. Collectively, our electric force is valued by the energy body, which some would liken it to our aura. When we accept that our physical body generates energy-the positive pole being our brain and the negative side being our coccyx (tailbone) and the nervous systems being outlets for electrical movement, then the associated electromagnetic field (or fields) should be present. Even some psychics consider our spirit bodies as models for our physical body.

Function of the Body Chakra.

We also have energy centers that run from the base up to the crown like dynamos along the central axis (spinal cord)-7 big chakras (Hindu word for energy wheels). Each of these chakras often produces electro-magnetic force whirlpools of differing vibration intensity or duration. Such various movements result in energy field layers that interlace with each other across our physical body.

The lowest movements (longer distances and slower oscillation) arise in our lower chakras-the Middle, the Sacra and the Solar Plexus, the higher the Head, Chest, Eye Brows (3rd Eye) and the Crown. Most of those charkas and their subdivisions tend to correspond to the Chinese acupuncture points and meridian schemes. Brief explanations of the seven charkas are: The Root Chakra is the First Chakra. (Gonad): Found between men's anus and scrotum, and women's anus and vaginal cavity. The roots are Conservation, Rooting, Support and Grounding. To interconnect with Earth is helpful. Its dimension is Earth (Chinese acupuncture point-Hui Yin.) This chakra is connected to our human energy field's first super-subtle body-the etheric stage (some term it the real body) The second chakra is the sacral or Dan Tian. (Lymphatic): position about one inch below the navel and one inch inwards towards the diaphragm. It's basis is feelings, individuality, impulses, and creativeness. The basic basis is the raw source of energy / power. The item it is is Wind. (Chinese acupuncture level-lower DanTian (Qihai) This chakra is linked to a region of emotional energy. (Emotional Body) The Solar Plexus is a Sixth Chakra. (Adrenal) The position is the main lung cavity, about 4 fingers from the naval press.

The base is that of personal power and metabolic capacity. The basic nature is the Will. The structure is focused on the very essence / being of one. Its parameter is Power. This chakra is in contact with the realm of mental energy. The fourth chakra is the heart (thymus): position about 2-3 inches above the solar plexus, roughly the sternum. It also roots to the heart organ and thus its region is the general area to the heart cavity between the upper lung cavity. Trust, Associations, Relationships, and Compassion are its foundation. It is the nature of interrelationships and everything that is in the realm of passion. The attribute is Water. (Chinese Acupuncture-Middle DanTian or ShungZhong) This chakra, the divine dimension boundary is associated with the astral energy field. (Intuitional / compassionate body) The Throat (Thyroid) is the fifth chakra: position between the skull and the lower neck cavity is about a midway point. From the mouth it is about one inch inwards. For guy, it's approximately the Adam's apple spot. The spinal cord is in regular vertical alignment. Communication and Creativity are its base. Vibration, concentration and guiding is nature.

The parameter is Tone.

This is connected to our area of etheric prototype energy.(will / spirit body or atmic core.) The Sixth Chakra is the Third Eye (Pituitary): position is the brain's central cavity. It is based on the faculty of perception, and everything that is driven by the imagination. It's the connection we view the higher zones and higher planes from. The nature resides within the subconscious and astral realms. Its dimension is Light (Chinese acupuncture point-Ying Dong.) This is related to the celestial energy field (soul stage or monadic body) The Seventh Chakra is the Crown (Pineal): it is situated at the top of the skull's pivot axis. It is where three skull plating, frontal lobe, left and right hemispheres converge. Its base is awareness, facts, and understanding. It's raffined thought. The nature of that is blissfulness. An aspect is Thinking (Chinese acupuncture-Upper DanTian or Bai Hui. This is related to the energy field of the Ketheric Model. (Divine body) Thus, as illness happens, it first influences the energy field-causing imbalances or blockages and in turn affects the normal functioning of the chakras which are in turn closely linked to our endocrine systems and indirectly to the environment.

Chinese Theory Of Qi

As described above, Chi's Chinese concept often falls into this human energy field paradigm-the meridians becoming outlets for Chi's motions and the viscera and organs bound to / connected by those meridians. Consequently, a steady and unblocked river of Chi or energy connotes that our viscera and vital organs function properly, and the opposite implies otherwise.

Therefore, to have a balanced physical body one needs a healthy body of resources. In order to heal a physical body, one must also first cure the energy system-removing the blockages and imbalances or harmful energies in order to prevent the physical body from degenerating and to enable it to regenerate. This would be a supplement to Western medicine.

Meditation to be able to access the energy system of our bodies, our usual sensory abilities need to be expanded-particularly our ability to feel the subtle sensations. All chi-kung and meditation (in addition, they are inter-related) will help you to keep your body and mind calm before you improve your ability to something outside your natural sensory skill. You should be able to feel the intensity of energy at one level-just like you might experience heat and cold. You can sense the flow of energy within the body and outside it. You begin to experience the body's thoughts of energy blockages, or energy shortages. You start to feel what is good energy and negative energy-take the different feeling of being in a Church and being in a Casket business for example.

Upon studying how to sense electricity, you start learning how to control it; how to remove bad energy, and how to substitute or replace it with good strength. You'll also note that our minds will direct the energy movements. Have you ever noticed that whenever you feel pain, the places where pain happens actually send messages to our brain, our central nervous system-that they need help and ask for soothing energies to be amplified to save them. Additionally, the brain will, of example, submit white blood cells to combat the bacteria or virus invasions, or red blood cells to do the repair work.

So meditation not only calms your mind, encourages the body to relax and heal, but also enables you to gain the ability to reach beyond and control the energy flows. The key to successful meditation is focusing; the ability to keep the various emotions at bay in order to attain concentration / mindfulness. The Chinese put it this way: "Replace with a single thought thousands of feelings." In addition to the ability to feel the invisible energy universe, advanced meditation often teaches you to decipher the aspects of the environment-you begin to perceive in your inner mind which shapes or interpretations the different energy around you is. Like ghosts and spirits, for example, without the physical body they live on energy bodies. They may refuse to believe that they are dead and have no physical body. Yet then their consciousness bodies will dematerialize and disappear into other realms, just like their physical body. We would be able to feel and see ghosts and spirits while our senses are heightened due to advanced meditative experience.

Feeling of Energy Vibration

I used to teach my students how to feel the vibrations of electricity. One approach that I often use is to teach them how to sense the sensations of various quartz forms. I'd try to open their hand charkas by concentrating my attention on their hands if they can't feel the stones. The left hand seems to be able to sense energy better, perhaps because the left side of the body is controlled by the right brain hemisphere. Hopefully explained by the fact that our right brain lobe regulates our ability to learn about arts as opposed to the left brain that manages our ability to know about science and mathematics topics... As the students progressed in their classes, I had them program their emotions into the quartz and tried to catch the different sensations that reflected the feelings of happiness or sorrow. I also showed them how to focus themselves by controlling their pulse and doing some meditative exercises to improve their capacity to feel strength.
As stated, one could feel the energy of emotions in the air at a higher level-one would be able to discern moods of joy, aggression or sadness as soon as one enters a room.

Even after the players vacated the space, one could sense the aftermath / residue of a violent encounter. Unlike abstract thought-forms, impulses are also forces and have definite and distinctive vibration levels. Many emotions are negative-for instance rage, sorrows or concerns-and their densities in our fields of energy create blockages in the inflow of positive energies. Consequently, prolonged exposure to these mental waves contributes to illness such as obesity, depression or asthma.

All these unorthodox extrapolations will help us aware that an all-round solution-the comprehensive form of healing-is required to restore oneself. Western medicine is a must, but it is insufficient in itself to insure the victims are fully recovered. Not only the body but also mind and spirit must be restored. Not onlydoes one subdue the signs but also locate and eradicate the root causes of sickness.

When a person gains mastery over energy control, he also begins to develop the capacity to not only experience his own energy but also to learn to perceive the energies of other individuals.

Either consciously or otherwise, he picks up certain body vibrations — including their painful symptoms and mental states. This will be the point when he starts to be impacted as he sits next to people suffering from illness-like chest pains and headaches for example. There is some sort of sympathetic resonance occurring at the point where force fields of two individuals intercede. Healers who do energy healing will always have this issue of being affected by their patients' powers, and if they do not do proper grounding and cleaning during and after the healing sessions, with prolonged exposure to their patients, they will pick up the same sicknesses.

Energy channeling

In addition to the ability to sense energy, the human often acquires the ability to channel energy. He will transfer energy into his body, and radiate it out of his hands for healing. Or, he can cause his body to become a mental medium for higher spiritual energies which he and others can project out to heal. Through his increased imagination ability he can conjure up modes of thought to do his bidding. Example: he will produce etheric hands or other items of energy such as etheric plasma balls or pyramids and will conduct specific tasks with them.

The individual may be so attuned to energy sensing at another higher level that he gains the communication gift-the ability to perform remote sensing and healing. Not only is space no longer a barrier but he can also try to reverse in order and heal the root causes of illness. Example: if the root cause of the disease is inserted during the day of a person's youth, he can imagine those early years psychologically and conduct healing on the person's picture in that period.

Spirit Vibration And Divination

Moving a little further, you can even do "divination" or commonly called fortune telling- the power to predict things by tuning into the spirit (astral) spatial vibrations. Pendulum use is but one case. Depending on which way the pendulum swings you will potentially get a "Yes" or "No" reaction to your past or future query about something unknown. One can also ask questions within the inner mind by searching for small physiological changes in your body, and get a "good" or "bad" answer. I take note of the movements in the chakra of the crown (pineal gland) to connote a "yes" and in the chakra of the inner third eye (pituitary gland) to get answers to my questions.

The Chinese name the Yang Dragon (Yang) the crown chakra (PaHui), and the Yin Tiger the 3rd Eye chakra (Ying Tong). The world of our subconscious mind is also the area we come across during dreaming. Many psychics in their visions have their prognoses or divination, or what we term the astral realm. Many people call the ability to predict or foresee things as insight or some call it a pure coincidence. But if they are replicated too often by mere coincidence, one should take a serious second look at this remarkable capacity.

On Mediums

Another subject most people are fascinated by is mediumship. Throughout my mind, one medium is one that causes him to be taken over by another person and replaced by another. We the come in the forms of god, angels, and divine leaders or even lower elemental spirits, or entities that are discarnated. With the medium's permission, an energy force will join the physical body of the human, usually through the chakra of the back throat, and briefly take shelter inside. For a certain period of time he gains control over the physical body of the human and his consciousness.

The medium will show extraordinary psychic abilities during this period-foretelling past and future occurrences, kinetically moving objects or performing exorcisms and so on. The Chinese pugilistic art has a divine fighting school where the warrior invokes the lord and calls it to his body to help him become victorious in battling and preventing him from being injured by his rivals. Many people who are desirous of good luck will use this platform for blessings.

I do notice that these mediums will usually crumble and become very frail after completing certain rituals and abandoning them after their visitors from out of this universe. I don't believe anything is safe and mediums pay a high price, as far as their wellbeing is concerned or the effects of future incarnations could be karmic. I was contacted by very strong mediums who offered to train me in a medium car, but all these proposals I politely declined. Nonetheless, I believe there is a difference between a mystic who communicates with his guides and a messenger who invokes ghosts, angels, and other forces of nature to join his body to conduct divination and to do his other offers. I often believe there are good and bad mediums; it all depends on whether the ceremonies they conduct are ulterior motives for their personal / mercenary intentions, or whether they provide a sincere service to help those in need.

Energy And Geomancy (Fengshui)

Feng Shui, Geomancy is also about energy-energy generated by the climate, gravitational powers and tides, seasonal fluctuations, celestial and planetary effects and static body placement in the environment. Another factor to consider is how your own body's energy copes with and resonates with all of these energy sources. Feng Shui's western application is to carry an assortment of scientific equipment to a location to check the different energy sources in the field. If you are energy sensitive, you will actually feel the power of "Feng Shui"-the good and bad "Qi"-rather than relying entirely on the masters ' learned Feng Shui concepts.

Most of us in lotteries or online events have strong cravings for good fortune or windfall. Hence, a fundamental understanding of how cultivating a healthy and constructive mindset can bring about material success, as well as good health and a harmonious partnership, is advantageous. Some who claim the energy will play a part in gaining luck would go to celestial masters for blessings. My energy consultancy company is targeted at clearing out negative energy blockage, supplanting my clients with positive energy and calming the seven big chakras. I frequently plan counseling workshops that demonstrate how to meditate , appreciate their body energy system and even control it. Between Peacock Ore's and other spiritual healing properties is its power to personally cleanse and detoxify each of the Chakras. Once each Chakra is thoroughly cleaned, Peacock Ore then immediately aligns all of the energy centres. As you and your energy centers merge for optimal health and vitality, the entire physical body and all your energy fields and organs are also balanced and synchronized with one another. Fluorite is another amazing mineral which has the power to sync your entire physical, mental and emotional energy bodies with the energy fields of your Aura and Ethereal.

Gather a large specimen of Peacock Stone, a good sized piece of Fluorite, and your Transparent Quartz healing crystals to begin self-healing. Put soft music on the soundtrack to replace the noise of the ego-mind, helping you to release all the pressures of the day.

Place it face-up on a flat surface. Place the Peacock Ore on your Crown Chakra, Fluorite on your Solar Plexus and keep your healing crystals Clear Quartz in your pockets. Note that the crystal on your left faces your hand, while the one on your right faces your fingertips outwards.

Visualize white light start flowing down into your Crown Chakra into the Peacock Ore and through your body all the way to your feet and flowing down through Mother Earth. Rest in the stillness for a few moments and continue to imagine simple, calm and rotating each of your energy centers in complete harmony with each other. The Fluorite put on your Solar Plexus begins infusing your physical body and energy centres, absorbing and aligning your whole Be-ness.

Once you've finished your self-healing therapy session, try to refresh the crystals and minerals by rinsing them in cool water for a few hours before sticking them in the Light. This easy, but highly effective method is most successful at least once a week when completed. If you are a healer or Light-Worker, you may choose to use this self-healing approach more often.

Having your emotions healthy is very critical to your overall health, enabling you to receive messages and instructions far better from Angels and from Spirit.

The Eastern philosophy and medicine of the Body's Energy Centres, rooted in ancient India and China, has historically treated body systems as inseparable and the life cycles taking place inside them. Their vocabulary remains halfway between structure and function, and describes those forces in the human body that reflect the movement of life energy and, in some ways, conduits for that flow that do not conform to Western science and medicine accepted anatomic frameworks.

The chakras are the sources of energy in the biological field of an individual and are responsible for their physiological and psychological state as well as for certain classes of organs. All of the human body's vital functions are defined by the force that revolves within the chakras. These can be described as "referred to as whirlpools," and in Indian, they are called "energy bursts" or "wheels." Exactly in these centers the cycle of energy transition occurs. Vital energy circulates in the chakras around the meridians together with blood, which powers all organs and processes in the human body. The human body is vulnerable to various disorders when the movement in those meridians stagnates. An excellent prevention technique, specifically designed to combat such deflation, is Chi Shot, an ancient Chinese self-healing system that triggers the energy centers. Chi Gun teaches people to unleash the tension by massaging specific areas that relate to the individual chakras themselves.

There are 49 chakras listed in the Vedic Canons, of which seven are fundamental; 21 are in the second circle, and 21 are in the sixth. According to the Vedis there are several sources of energy flowing from the chakras to different locations. Three of these canals are important.

The first, named "shushumna," is empty, embedded within the spine. The other two energy channels, "ida" and "pingala," are on either side of the spine. In most countries these two networks are the most involved whereas "shushumna" stagnates.

The seven fundamental chakras turn in the stable individual's body at high speeds but slow down in periods of disease or advancing age. The Chakras stay partially open when the body is in a harmonious state. Closed chakras can not obtain energy which contributes to different disorders.

The first simple chakra, "Muladhara," is found in the tailbone region, at the base of the spine. Life energy is stored in this chakra which is at the heart of a strong and healthy immune system. Until wasting his or her stores of this vital energy it is impossible for a person to become ill, aged or even die. Muladhara regulates that very will for survival. The bones and limbs, the jaws, the hair, the urinogenital network and the large intestine are also in control. The first signs of a malfunctioning Muladhara are unreasonable fear, fatigue, lack of security or trust in the future, trouble with the legs and feet and intestinal disorders.

The Muladhara chakra's disrupted operation triggers energy shortage, digestive problems, skeleton and spine illnesses and nervous stress among others.

The second chakra, called "Svadhistana," is found at the sacrum point, three or four fingers below the button on the abdomen. The pelvis, kidneys and sexual functions are controlled by this chakra. Through this chakra we even feel the feelings of other peoples. Symptoms of the "Svadhistana" dysfunction include renal disorders, cystitis and arthritis.

The third chakra, "Manipura," is found in the area around the solar plexus. This chakra is the core where the energy produced by digestion and breathing is processed and transmitted. It is responsible for hearing, gastro-intestinal tract, kidneys, gall bladder, pancreas, and nervous system. The above are the signs of a dysfunctional "Manipura": heightened and persistent anxiety, as well as gastrointestinal, liver and nervous disorders.

The fourth chakra, "Anahata," is found in the chest area and is also considered the core chakra. Through this Chakra we produce and receive love.

It is liable for the liver, the lungs, the bronchi, the arms and the legs. Stagnation signs include fatigue, and physiological imbalances.

The fifth chakra, "Vishudha," is found at the throat stage and is the core of intellectual and rational competencies. This chakra sustains the flesh, sensory organs as well as the trachea and lungs. Symptoms include a lack of emotional control, cervical spine pain, soar throats, communication difficulties, and esophageal and thyroid disorders.

The sixth chakra, "Adjna," is situated between the brows of the body, and is considered the "third hand." "Adjna" circulates energy to the head and pituitary gland and is also responsible for determining our growth in peace. If the "third eye" of an individual ceases to function correctly, a decline in intellectual capacity, headaches and migraines, earaches, olfactory infections, and psychological disorders may be observed.

"Sahasrara," the seventh chakra, is located at the very top of the head and reflects the peak where the consciousness of a person vibrates with the highest frequency. It is called a sacred hub for cosmic energy and the entrance into the body.

A static "Sahasrara," as well as a lack of basic intelligence, may result in a reduction in or absence of inner wisdom.

With this basic knowledge of the first seven chakras, we will address the question: "How do we use this wisdom to find the roots of our troubles and difficulties, and learn to control the workings of the chakras for ourselves with the aid of Eastern Medicine?"

From the Eastern Medicine viewpoint our wellbeing relies on the dissemination of our knowledge area of energy-consciousness. An electricity deficit inevitably leads to illnesses. According to Tibetan Medicine, the only distinction between young and old, and between a sick and stable adult, is the difference in the whirlpool energy centers of the chakras ' rotational speed. If these differing speeds are controlled, the elderly will rejuvenate and the wounded will regenerate. So the best way to preserve and sustain our health, youth and prosperity is to establish and maintain a balanced energy core movement.

By a set of physical movements the best way to keep the chakras aligned is. Yannis didn't just name them activities but routines. Such routines allow the human body to shape its energy centers to an ideal functional level. The seven rituals, one for each chakra, have to be done together every morning and in the evening when not necessary. Skipping routines unbalances the allocation of time, and so you should skip no more than one day a week for the best results. The daily rituals of chakras are important not only to revitalize the body but also to achieve success in every facet of life. "You will become happier, too, until you know how to change your strength," Yannis concluded.

For know such traditions (which have changed the lives of many cultures throughout the world), it is much more important to see them in practice than to try to follow formal explanations or maps. A DVD, accessible from Helix 7, Inc., contains actual ritual examples.

Meditation is another way of keeping the chakras healthy, and in their optimum half-open state. Meditative approaches are fundamental to human experience; they have accrued through many different cultures over the centuries, and have proven their importance in achieving peace, unity, equanimity, and transcendent misery.

People who regularly meditate are typically calmer, healthier, wealthier, and more productive people. They are more successful in their daily lives as they make full use of their mental and physical capacity, skills and skill. All too often we people fail to realize the immense dormant forces in our bodies that are still unawakened. We need to know how to relive and use them. That can be done by reflection alone. More than 1000 years ago, Western people of knowledge, who considered meditation to be a critical need, staggered at this finding. We learned to use the strength of their brains to manipulate their internal organs and regulate their metabolism. Meditation is to the mind what meditation is to the body; it can build up mental strength just like physical force. Just as it is vital that an individual trains his or her body in sports, it is important that an individual exercises his or her mind by meditation.

Early morning is the best time to meditate, ideally at midnight. Do not meditate when you are depressed, angry, anxious or ill, as these intense emotional and physiological disturbances make it impossible for a calm state of mind.

It is best to prepare for a successful meditation session for the undistracted solitude of a peaceful, clean room with roses, or the calming noises of Mother Nature-near a lake, river, waterfall, woodland or fields.

Several different mental activities, rooted in ancient cultures, come under the common umbrella of "meditation." Such mental development approaches that include emotional and intellectual aspects, and may also be synchronized with specific movements.

Why You Need To Adjust The Chakras To Cope With a Modern Lifestyle

Chakra Centres, the energy vortices from which we control our energy flow, are constantly changing as they connect, rectify and sustain their complex energy balance. While each of us has a different pattern of prevailing chakras describing our particular energy flow, connected to each person and their individual lifestyle, the energy chakras often influence our minute-to-minute energy states as we conduct our daily activities. We can have reason to rest, become depressed, undertake physical activity or focus on life during an ordinary day and each requires a different energy source from the appropriate energy centres.

Definitions of chakras connected with certain activities are the correlation of the 1st and 2nd chakras with physical and functional occupations and behaviors, while the brow chakra is correlated with creative tasks and the solar plexus with interpersonal behavior.

Our rapidly shifting habits and multi-tasking implies that our chakra equilibrium is even more critical than ever and that sustaining complex relationships at work and socially involves a healthy heart chakra balance, but we can also be forced into a position where there is no such interaction or where our interpersonal abilities are not respected. It will help a lot to sustain our physical and mental well-being by managing our chakra centers this way.

While there is no concern when a single chakra has superiority, the disparity will lead other chakras to try to cover the positions of those underused and we will feel' out of order' as our emotions are controlled by incorrect energy centres. We get tired when this occurs and need a refresh.

Because the chakras work so dynamically as we conduct our daily tasks, it is necessary to periodically adjust them so that they are balanced for our energy system. Because we are all special there is no explanation for how to manage our individual chakras, but using crystals aligned with each energy core you can use a disciplined approach.

Crystals tend to intensify the chakra-related energies and there are correspondences correlated with each crystal that allow them to work best with a certain chakra. Through knowing the right crystals to use, controlling chakra energies can be balanced so you'll always feel energized and inspired.

For a desired effect there are new ways of charging crystals with certain energies, crystals charged in this manner will have an enhanced impact on the corresponding chakra resulting in a better, more positive energy balance. These are recognized as isochronic crystals, and they soon become the standard way of approaching the function of crystal energy.

Chapter 12: How To Maintain The Chakras

Balancing the chakra for recovery

With a powerful example of meditation, you can align one or all of the chakras and see how it will differentiate your wellbeing and performance.

It is commonly understood how meditation can improve your overall health and wellness, and make your mind calmer. Some background and understanding Chakra Meditation By proficient meditation, you can minimize tension and get a better sense of satisfaction.

A few times a day, exercise was given to change the brain and promote complex tasks. A few times a day. It is also used in an effort to achieve knowledge, an enhanced frame of mind, as a way to go beyond common thinking and presences.

Meditation will transfer the chakra energy by duplicating the chant for each chakra either on its own or in a sequence.

The chakra mechanism is an old device, recognized for thousands of years to many cultures.

Chakra (pronounced CHUK-ruh), in Sanskrit, means disk or rim. The cores are called channel-wheels in Tibetan Buddhism. Taoist yoga is a dynamic practice focused on the regulation and movement as vortexes of these essential forces.

Understanding and Balancing the Major 16 Chakras

Chakras are also called lotuses and offer us some sense of the chakras ' existence. The lotus with its beautiful flowers blooming on the water surface, under the illumination of the Sun (spirit), has its roots deep in the murky obscurity of the waters (the real one). The chakras can be locked, in bud, open or flowering, active or inactive, just like the lotus blossom.

The ancient western alchemical practice used the chakra method, with metals and planets allocated to the chakras in a complex communication scheme that formed the basis of the search for divine salvation by the alchemists. With alchemical arts diminishing, awareness of the chakras even diminished. In the late nineteenth and early twentieth centuries, belief in the chakras re-emerged in the West with the rise of the Theosophy movement.

The chakra system is an electrical network of data storage, much like a machine which many healers feel or see. It is the human body's mental gateway through the nervous system, our spirit body & the holographic network. The nervous system is our neural device, providing information and collecting from the chakras, interacting with all facets of the body. The chakras act as energy transmitters from one point to the next, transmitting qi or prana to the human body.

While there are many minor chakras in the body & at our joints, it is recognised that there are 7 main chakras between the groin and top of the head, with 2 others located about 18 inches above the top of the head, identified as the Soul Star, the Earth Star, about 18 inches below the foot. There are differences of opinion about where some of the smaller chakras are. I deal with & align 16 main chakras, from the Earth Star through to the Monad: Divine link, some of which are not recognised by other healers or structures, rendering my healing practice special.

For everything, our "I can believe it when I see it" mentality, which restricts the multi-sensory experiences of humans, personal experience is a crucial part of western tolerance. Nevertheless, there are many recorded incidences where, even after extensive medical tests, individuals have had physical pain, in the heart for example, with no apparent cause identified. When these people went on to have a crystal cure & chakra alignment, the therapist noticed that after the rebalancing, their suffering was healed to be related to a past life accident. Most healers claim that actual diets are embedded in mental and emotional imbalances and the mental and emotional structures must also be treated in order to heal the physical body.

Each of the 7 chakras that are generally known refers to a physical system and its associated organs and glands. Increasing chakra is allocated tone, colors and crystals although the colors and roles of each chakra varies greatly dependent on different traditions.

The First Chakra: Base Chakra situated at the base of the spine's coccyx region, refers to the adrenals, large intestines and rectum. It shares kidney duty with 2nd chakra.

This chakra is regarded as the fire of the kundalini or serpent; life force for the fight for survival, salvation or "death," social identification, bonding and loyalty. Expression of energy by the root chakra is directly related to the level of health of a person. The celestial fire that awaits release lies dormant until the higher self can fully harness the power of its physical & metaphysical life-level etheric energy source. The first chakra's message is that of Oneness, not division. Crystals: Garnet, Black Tourmaline, Dravite, Black Onyx, Smokey Quartz, Obsidian; and middle C.

The Second Chakra: Sacral Chakra is found at halfway between the public bone and naval (some beliefs see it in the naval), connected to the testes, prostate and ovaries. The pelvis is the Space & The Goddess visible image. The Hidden Feminine / Goddess Self anches here. It is the artistic core and refers to sensuality as well as attraction, strength (personal power when it's in equilibrium, & ego supremacy when it's unbalanced) and wealth or prosperity, ability to create & take risks, fight or flight, endurance, perseverance, & financial acumen. This is then our artistic hub, the center of our love and our individuality-being relaxed as a woman or a man with our body.

Shadow aspects: Controlling / disempowering or using others for your own gain.
Colour: orange; Note: D; Crystals: Amber, Carnelian, Tiger Eye.

The Third Chakra: Solar Plexus Chakra is pancreatic, kidney, gallbladder, thyroid, spleen, and digestion linked. It is here that our unresolved feelings are processed and that is why we' digest' our thoughts, or not! This chakra is about strength of will, self-esteem, self-discipline, determination, bravery, compassion, integrity & intuition, self-respect & self-honour. Shadow aspects: giving away personal elective authority out of approval; selfish conduct. Colour: yellow; note: e; crystals: citrine, sunstone, chrysophrase of lemon.

The Fourth Chakra: The heart chakra is found in the middle of the chest and refers to the heart and thymus gland. This is the chakra of self-and other-love, sympathy, and forgiveness. Aspects of shadow: envy, joylessness, anger and the failure to forgive. Colour: a pink mix, for self-love, & white, for esteem of others. Before we can love anyone, we must love ourselves first; Note: F; Crystals: Rose Quartz, Green Aventurine, Amazonite, Chrysophrase.

The Fifth Chakra: Throat Chakra is at the base of the chest, connected to the sound of the thyroid and parathyroid, and the neck. It relates to our ability to speak our own truth & trust, and is where we encourage love to reach our lives. It's where we are imposing our will over others or offering us our power / control. This is the cornerstone of confidence, understanding about yourself, moral integrity, and ability to keep the promise. Aspects of Shadow: An intense need to monitor interactions and activities. Color: gold; Note: G; Crystals: Larimar, Gold Lace Agate, Lapis, Aquamarine, Diamond Silica, Azurite / Malachite.

The Sixth: Brow Chakra is often considered the third eye, is situated between the brows of the head and just above them. It is linked to the pineal gland and divine perception, and the ability to articulate creativity and vision. Aspects of shadow: interpreting reality in a self-serving way. Note: A; Crystals: Amethyst, Sugilite, Kyanite, Azurite.

The Seventh Chakra: Crown Chakra is at the top of the head, and a line up from the tips of the ears and straight up from the tip of the nose can be seen by' drawing.' It refers to the pituitary gland and is our direct connection to the higher consciousness and the spirit. This is the source of confidence both in the Almighty and in inward direction, wisdom into salvation & the Divine commitment. Shadow aspect: the need to learn why things are happening as they are, which is what lets you live in the past. Colour: white; note: B; crystal: quartz black, selenite, quartz indigolite (blue).

I received the following knowledge from the Almighty several years ago during a healing session. As I have been practicing with these chakras my perception of them has through. The Eighth Chakra, also known as the Soul Star or Interpersonal Chakra, is somewhat familiar to people. Less is learned around Nine to Twelve Charkas. Data differs with regard to the higher dimensions. That is because individuals are at various levels of consciousness, which hold different degrees of vibration. You can only see the truth based on where you are currently looking from.

The 5 Higher Chakras, 8-12 These 5 higher charkas were disconnected eons ago and are now being reconnected to Spirit through our release. The cycle can be intensified through an Initiation of Ascension.

The higher charka's colors vary from person to person & depending on your particular intent or role as a spirit. Crystals: Herkimer & Tibetan Diamonds, White Quartz, Selenite, Indicolite (Blue Tourmaline in Quartz), Moldavite, Cavansite, Apophyllite, Prehnite, double ended.

The Eighth Chakra: Soul Star which is also known as the Transpersonal Chakra is about 18 inches above the heart. This is the nucleus that houses all of our lifelong relationships & deals, karmic relations, etc. The Soul Star of an individual overlaps with that of the individuals with whom they have had long-term relationships or sexual encounters, and they do not separate entirely on their own, although the pair the physically disconnect. Therefore, it is very important to be able to cancel all those old relationship arrangements so as to make it easier for new potential partnerships to come to you, or to clear a path for your current relationship, helping it to develop more entirely. The eight chakras are also the source of isolation, staying in the present moment, absolute trust, recognition of unconscious direction and the capacity to detect perception. It's the core of higher intellect. It represents the domain where the spirit mergs with the Supreme Consciousness.

It also marks the point at which the spirit reflects itself into flesh, into the body of human beings. Reference to: C;

The Ninth Chakra: This incarnation's intergalactic doorway to the Almighty and the BluePrint, & our Higher Emotional Core. This is where we keep all the knowledge on who we will be & become, in this current incarnation-our eye color, hair color, certain traits, attributes of personality & what we will be / do in this lifetime. The knowledge is becoming our DNA. Once we move into this life we have all of this. The Model may look broken, weakened or shattered, divided, scratched, scattered or even distributed during a healing process. I interacted with a very sad lady, so I felt she didn't want to be here. Once I told her, She confirmed that. Her plan actually appeared fragmented or broken and I believe if she hadn't had the consultation with me she would have tried to leave anyway. When I called for a fresh model to be brought in she burst into tears and she felt completely changed after the session. She had a huge release especially when I was clearing her ninth and eleventh chakras. Note: D The Tenth Chakra: Interdimensional Portal to the Soul is the portal to all the other encounters (and dimensions) that we have had in the world.

This chakra is where the spirit itself splits and scatters all over the world, causing' retrieval.' Once all facets have been restored, the individual has full access to all the infinite possibilities of who they were and who they are— their' common archetypes' for want of a better term. In putting within one chakra the nature of those facets or parts of consciousness, it gives us the ability to work with all of our talents and abilities. Many people have access to only one to ten of their universal archetypes, and that's quite restricting because we have an infinite number in reality. Note: E The Onceth Chakra: Universal Portal to the Divine is where, so to say, duality starts. It's the' area of convergence' between Light and Dark where we have all the contracts and agreements that relate to our spirit, while the eighth chakra is the contracts and agreements of this current incarnation. Clearing the eleventh chakra is essential in equilibrating an individual and giving them full access to their Divinity. I consider the obstacles in the eleventh chakra most definitely conflict with our Divine link. This is where our Occult, Black Magic & the Abyss contracts are kept. We all have parts of ourselves that have felt darkness, for that is part of the journey of the Soul to discover Light and Dark, Order & Disorder.

For us part of the Divine plan is to observe Duality — Light and Dark, and all the rainbow beams in between. Often I consider this chakra to be very imbalanced and may need a considerable Love injection, & maybe a' fresh' chakra to render by need. When I clear people sometimes encounter an immediate change with this chakra, and they remark that instantly they feel different, more linked to the Divine. Note: F The Twelfth Charka: Monadic Soul Scale Completing the five higher Charkas is the 12th Chakra or the Monad is called the Divine's individualized Spirit-Spark & is often referred to as the I am Presence. The Monad is often believed to be the Soul's Ascended Master Degree. Each single Monad or Spirit-Spark produces & is split into 12 Souls pairs. A pair is known as TwinFlames. The Monad is often regarded as the stage of Soul's Ascended Master or Spirit. When cleared I see the TwinFlame of the individual as well as their Divine Ray- their unique Divine taste, in the brightness of light, which is their' feature' as Spirit. Here's the Soul's BluePrint, the TwinFlame of the Soul — twin-self or miroir opposite. Occasionally, I see here the souls of other essential ties. It's a relation where the Monad and the God don't vary.

I often see the two BluePrints — the Soul & this incarnation — reflect each other. The same heterogeneity also occurs in each one. If there is a break in the Blueprints, this applies in fact to a disconnection of our being's male and female facets. The most important step toward achieving Harmony is unifying the male / female energies within us.

If there is a difference between the male / female elements, it may lack one half of BluePrint. So the Monad is present but they usually miss their TwinFlame. Their TwinFlame steps in by getting the BluePrint back together and rendering it whole, and the customer has recourse to interacting with their mirror-self. Note: F #The following is based on my own numbering system to include the other essential chakras with which I operate. The numbers are not significant, where the chakras are & what they are' doing' is: The Thirteenth Chakra: Divine Heart Space / Star Tetrahedron Heart Center: positioned halfway between the Throat & Heart Chakras, above the Thymus, this is the chakra of Co-Creative Divine Consciousness, Divine Internal Acceptance, Unconditional Love & Compassion for Self & Others.

Wellness is theoretically an integral part of our experience as we wake this center. Everything takes purpose and satisfaction, and we experience the joy of love that comes out of this chakra.

This core is one Single Chakra when completely powered. This is vital because you can then align your physical, physiological, mental & spiritual bodies with a single chakra, and harmonize their strength. Operating with the united chakra you unify the five higher & the ten lower chakras into one so that they all work according to the strength of unconditional love-based energy flowing through this Divine-Heart center.

The gland of Thymus regulates the immune system & our ageing process. When the physical body (glands & organs) uses the thymus-governing imprint it is fully functional. Obviously the thymus is getting smaller as we mature. You hold that disabled by tapping the thymus regular. Many initiations are said to hold the thymus active as well & that after initiation you can avoid ageing. One such initiation is Reiki, particularly after level II.

When the Spiritual flow is more clear & strong, we may travel regularly in accordance with the Purpose of Spirit across life.

Then as male (thought) & female (emotions) are no longer antagonistic, it will continue to develop a proper hormone balance. Colour: depends on the intent of the soul; Note: F #The Fourteenth Chakra: Quantum-Holographic Portal to the Sacred is between the knees & is where the Cosmic Holographic Internet binds to the real. The Network is like a highway that links us to everybody in the World & all. Through the Internet, we often have unwanted relations with others & give away our strengths & abilities to cover. Healing energy can be guided through the Network to restore the Computer, and thus cure the' organic' body — which only seems strong but is still water. If the physical body gets damaged, the Internet often gets damaged — torn or split. Colour: Green-White Note: B The Fifteenth Chakra: Spiritual Portal to the Sacred is between the feet, at the ankle point, & grounds & binds energy to the physical plane. When this core is triggered we feel connected to Mother Earth & feel one with her strength, & that of all forms of life — referred to as All My Connections by native Americans. Environmental awareness remains here & our desire to support our Mother Earth. Color: Navy Blue; Notice A The Sixteenth Chakra: Earth Star is about 18 inches below our feet & when triggered, our Soul-Self shifts completely into the real into the Ultimate Moment of the Now, where we are the most strong-Spirit witnessing person. We can't be anything but Spirit, but people tend to ignore this Reality, and there's nothing to search for except inside themselves-to note that we're a bit of the Divine. Color: Forest Green; Note A #These 16 chakras together with other major & minor chakras shape the most powerful connection between our physical and spiritual bodies. The chakras interact directly with our nervous system, hence the significance of clearing all systems— physical bodies & electricity. We see hints as to what chakras are out of control as we analyze our habits (attitudes, principles & beliefs). There are many methods of visualizing to get the charkras into harmony & alignment and in my experience they need to be done every day.

Physical pain associated with imbalances in the chakra is very true. Having worked with people for over 20 years as a shaman and healer, I've seen many cases in which physical pain was removed or resolved during a healing session. I find we're primarily holding our history in our backs, which reflects our background — practically behind us! People also encounter a physical feeling correlated with a' torn' hand.

They can experience pain between the shoulder blades in their mid-spinal area, and when they imagine their emotional heart, either 'see' a picture of something that covers their heart (e.g., a box or a cage) or 'see' it as damaged. If a person has problems with money and feels discouraged in some area of their life, they can experience low backache.

Over the years my research has developed into my own process, Micro-Fusion Holographic Healing, which combines Shamanic healing techniques as well as the many modalities in which I have learned. I found the body reacting to this gentle research by freeing & opening itself to the Spirit-Self in a very gentle but profound manner.

In this final part of The Chakras, I wanted to address some concerns & problems that have frequently come up with customers over the years, including some of the forms that I find most helpful for holding the chakras in harmony.

At the end of their session customers told me to 'cover my chakras' and this is a very critical issue to address. This also sometimes emerges as a question: "Should I leave my chakras open or closed?" Other healers have told clients they need to shut their chakras in order to be 'safe.' And since my customers know that I'm opening all charkas and getting them into sync and then offering my customers a diagram to hold their chakras intact, this creates confusion obviously.

The chakras are basically mini machines, collecting and storing information which is then passed through the nervous system and subtle structures to their controllers, the physical & spirit bodies. It's like trying to operate your machine with it switched off when your chakras are locked. It is therefore not a defense, but the reverse, to leave you vulnerable and exposed to harmful or unwelcome energies.

Once your chakras are accessible & work in accordance with each other, you connect with your Spirit-Self openly. Most notably, your heart chakra is active while your charkas are up, and you are exuding Love in and around you, and this is your biggest defense.

The next question I get the most asked is, "How do I hold my chakras open?" One thing I find is that all the other chakras are impacted when the Earth Star is closed or deactivated. Some chakras are partially open, but sluggishly travel, some chakras are closed. Conversely I find that all chakras are also influenced favorably when the Earth Star is then raised.

To go through how to open & sustain your chakras, first we need to decide how they move-in what direction. There are 2 key theories about how the chakra mechanism works-if that is your view, both are true & function. The method you've been trained first is usually the one that fits for you. My Crystal Master taught me this way: Each chakra spins the opposite direction to the next one, forming a DNA-like spiral that binds them together, beginning with the Earth Star rotating in the counter-clockwise direction. Another simple way to remember is that all the odd numbers rotate in clockwise direction, while even numbers turn counter in clockwise direction.

Where you test this is with a pendulum, which is also how the chakras are transparent & free. You should place a pendulum over any chakra, and inquire to see how it works. When a chakra is locked, there is nothing the pendulum will do. If the pendulum is only partially open it will move very slowly. The pendulum can swing effortlessly & relatively quickly in a large circle when a chakra is fully open. Once you've decided whether your Earth Star is open or closed, and your solar plexus & heart chakras have been tested, you can start realigning all of your chakras.

For this exercise it is safest to sit in a chair, so you have easy access to all your chakras. Beginning with the Planet Star, which is approx. You aim your pendulum 18 cm below your foot at the chakra. Step forward & lean on your thigh with your elbow. This will give you the right spot, at your ankles level & forward from them. Now do counter-clockwise pendulum turn. Do this for about 30 seconds, until the pendulum quickly swings by itself.

Continue up to your ankle chakra— clockwise, then knees— against clockwise, first chakra at the base of the spine— against clockwise, and so on, keeping the pendulum over the region of each chakra until you get to the crown chakra on top of your head that turns in clockwise direction.

At this stage I realize you question how you're going to clear the higher charkas. Because purpose is all, you'll imagine bringing each of them down before you— out of your body at about your core chakra. Start with the 8th chakra— contra-clockwise, and so on into the 12th chakra. Let through one spin until they can spin spontaneously without your support. At the end stay still for a few minutes, your eyes closed to remember how you felt. See if you feel different from the way you did before starting this exercise. Will you feel more relaxed, more at peace?

Another technique you can use to unlock each chakra is to imagine each rotating in the right direction and to visualize the acceptable color for each one. Another option is to keep over each chakra a double ended transparent quartz crystal or selenite wand while using the pendulum. Alternatively, between your thumb & index fingers, you should keep a Herkimer or Tibetan Diamond at the ends. That will help clear every chakra more completely of any unwelcome energies. Ideally there should be daily practice of chakra balancing.

Chapter 13: Experiences After The Opening Of The Third Eye

The sixth chakra is situated between the two ears, namely the third eye chakra called Ajna in Sanskrit, which allows the lips and eyes their first shrinkage, distorting the orientation of the jaws and thus causing all the vision problems.
The human species has the ability to smile which no other animal has.
But the development was still not complete.
The human race had not yet fully stood on its two.
The development begins!
But this time, it's not just an accidental human development taking place on its own; as it does in the case of livestock.
Actually, the tool of creation is gray matter today, which was given to the human species when it was on its two hands.
We haven't been fully up on our two though. We have yet to!
How?
Look at the stages of human evolution in its creation.
Together with the passing of various sequential periods through development, in every next step of it, human species has gone straighter and straighter.
We paid the price of partly opening the two higher chakras by having our five animal chakras partially closed as we arrived on our two's.
Now we have to complete this evolution by opening all our 7 chakras in one go with the aid of the gray matter that has endowed us with only this evolution!
Everything is human! One by one!
It's because this time the aware gray matter, and not the latent genetics, will do so!
And then there won't be any more issues with eye ight, body health and mental safety!
The latest development will be more a revolt than a pure evolutionary automated evolution!

Now we have achieved such a stage of evolution simply by being on our two's that if we fully open our five animal chakras, the two higher chakras, namely Ajna (third eye chakra) and Sahasrara (crown chakra) unlock themselves!
Not even that much is expected. If we fully open only one chakra, the remaining six of them, including Ajna (the third eye chakra), will be opened alone!
Now, compare this definition of Ajna (third eye chakra) with my personal experience of opening it while interacting with a lady whose upper chakras like Anahata, Vishuddha and Ajna were more influenced than her lower ones, i.e., Muladhara, Svadhisthana, and Manipura. The following were the scenes where we left with her Anahata and Vishuddha last two times while working.

The first session had finished as follows: I told her to sustain this pose for a few days before we could move on with our body's interference in mind relations.

She came back with the accusation of thinking she had gone undressed in part while leaving her eyes loose.

"Anahata is doing this to us. Vishuddha is going to do this even further. Are you ready for the next step?"-I replied.

She stopped for a couple of seconds.

She held her shoulders wide open throughout her pause; which gave her bust a beautiful body-lift though still a slight one.

She looked right into my lips.

She took care not to let it pinch her back again.

And then she said-" Yeah, I'm happy. "Next we were to go from Anahata to Vishuddha.

The second session concluded as follows: she had concentrated on her HARA-about two inches below her maritime.

Her body looked like a beauty model personified in the very shape of Venus!

"Are you ready to proceed from here to the next stage, the opening Vishuddha took you in?"-I questioned.

This period, she had not taken much breath.

"Yeah, I am happy."-Her reply came straight away.

We were to go from Vishuddha to open Ajna (third eye) next.

The current session went like this: I told her to pay attention to her foot now, this period.

She has.

"Where do you expect the weight to settle on the top of your feet?"-I told her.

She couldn't comment straight away.

I told her to switch to her usual old pose, which she did.

"Where do you find the weight on the bottom of your foot to be sitting now?"-I told her again.

"On the sides of the outside!"-she felt this moment.

"Come up again to the new pose and inform me now!"-I had in my speech a sense of urgency and immediacy.

This succeeded and she could feel the difference instantly.

"Now it's the inside margins, more towards the big toe!"-she yelled, crying.

"Just search, what is up to your jaws!"-I had the same excitement in my accent.

She looked lost yet again.

I told her again to go back to her old, usual pose, which she immediately did.

"In terms of their compatibility with each other, test your jaws now."-I sent her the advice.

"Hey, the lower jaw lies behind the upper one, up... under it."-she offered the dental geometry terms.

"Go back to the new pose and inform me now!"-I had a sense of pressure and immediacy in my speech again.

She did, and immediately told the difference, "The lower jaw has fallen forward as well as down; or I can even tell, the upper jaw has gone backwards as well as up a bit. It's putting pressure on my jaws." "What's that feeling of pressure like?"-I was eagerly waiting for her response.

Like Strength! Energy going into my denture and into my eyes from there!"She screamed with a great joy peeping out of her lips. Her eyes were shouting E-N-E-R-G-Y! Her eyes were oozing E-N-E-R-G-Y!" That's the opening of Ajna (third eye chakra). We need to move on from Ajna to Sahasrara (the crown chakra) which is the lord of all of them! Are you ready to travel further?"I questioned her desire to go beyond Ajna (third eye chakra) and her readiness to go beyond it.""Immediately her reaction was this time. From Ajna, we were to go on to Sahasrara (the crown chakra) next! Doesn't this tale give the exact definition of Ajna (the third eye chakra) in a more day-to-day language? Ajna (the third eye chakra) is opened clearly if we stand on our two's correctly!

Vision treatment activates not only the Ajna (third eye chakra) but all the 7 chakras in one go through a very slight on - off turn in the body, since they are all anatomically and physiologically related in the human species.

G B Singh is an electronics engineer by education, enthusiastic about improving quality of life on earth.

He also decided to train people in the immediate vision correction technique, free of charge, by automatically raising their third eye.

He is also focusing on a techno-scientific project called Virtual Reality Machine with the goal of technologically mechanizing the biological process of dissolving all body musculature rigidities so that almost all lifestyle disorders can be removed in one hour for real, for life; for which he wants volunteer members from all over the world and has already called for it.

Conclusion

The third eye chakra is number six, and is situated between the brows in the center of the forehead, so it is sometimes also regarded as the brow chakra.
The hue is a deep blue Indigo. While blue is the color of contact with others, indigo transforms the blue inward, offering deep insights and immediate comprehension to enhance personal thought. Indigo symbolizes peace of heaven.
Too much indigo and we believe that we are too far above others, and that we live in a fantasy world.
The Sanskrit word, Ajna means both "the core of awareness" and "the center of order." Intuitive understanding or gratitude is one concept of perception and that sums up this center of control. It is awareness and understanding, but it has something innate to it. This is what binds the inner and outer realms.
The source of energy is at the core of our moral vision.

This chakra sees beyond the body in the context of clairvoyance, telepathy, insight, vision, creativity, and imagining to where we get knowledge, distinguishing fantasy from reality, creating art, and seeing auras.
It is linked to awareness, thinking, vision, intelligence, memory, nervous system, lips, mouth, nose, pineal gland, pituitary gland. They may suffer brain tumors, deafness, coma, epilepsy, learning difficulties, anxiety, paranoia, panic attacks, insomnia and isolation when it's unbalanced.
When you suffer from depression, be cautious to have too much indigo as it may push you further into the depression, focus instead on the chakra of the heart and neck, and this will immediately begin to open and stabilize it.
Lapis, Blue Jasper and Blue Sodalites are the stones to support this energy core.
Nature pictures to use for opening and calming this chakra are the atmosphere of the night just after sunset before it becomes dark.
To remove this Chakra, we need to protect a child's innocence by getting away from the cynical approach of seeing what we want to see, to continue seeing and feeling it as though it were the first time. Don't bother using the phrase "is" For examples ' Indigo is the color of this chakra' instead of saying' Indigo seems to be the color of this chakra.' The best way to keep the third eye open is to make sure you have enough energy going through it from the chakra immediately below it. Take time to look into the early evening skies and do deep breathing exercises.
We are now near the end of our trip through the chakras-at the chakra of the third eye (also regarded as the brow chakra), which is in the middle of the forehead. Now, at the end of the journey in the territories of the sixth and seventh chakras, we are in the spiritual realm-where it transcends the concept of a different entity.

The brow chakra is aligned with the head, mouth, nose and sinuses, and certain functions of the brain. Third-eye chakra conditions include those of the brain, ears and nose as well as headaches and migraines, and illnesses of the nervous system.

This chakra is about how we feel what's going on in our lives. We perceive our life events simply and without background distractions when we are healthy here. They think clearly, without getting caught up in self-destructive or pessimistic learning loops. We are also intuitive, able to count on this insight and trust it, and feel connected with our spiritual beliefs.

Obviously we have a long history of devaluing this more feminine, natural form of being in the universe in the West. It is the more pragmatic masculine way of thinking that is highly valued in our culture. This means that many of us have a strong ability to make use of our analytical and rational brains, which is really good of course. However, we'll become unbalanced without learning the appropriate "softer" cognitive skills. And that's why we still feel out of control of our racing thoughts, concepts and ambitions, and our mind is still "whirling" around sometimes when we want to rest, even sometimes when we're asleep.

There are many ways to work for this chakra to level out. It is very good to work with visual art, color, and painting. Similarly, basic meditation is pleasant-simply focusing on the air, enabling thoughts to come and go, and not interacting with it. This practicing on the cushion of meditation can then transfer over into our daily lives, and we become less connected with our emotions, more in contact with our intuitive selves, and our running mind may slow down in time.

Mind regeneration and EFT are very effective ways to balance out the chakra of the third eye. It's often the case we don't see things plainly in our current lives because we see them from the background through a lens. When we have been criticized as an infant, as an individual, we can foresee criticism anywhere. If we were not allowed to express ourselves as a teenager, we might feel unable to do so as an adult, and if we do, we may feel unheard of. An inner child therapy session or an EFT (Emotional Liberation Technique) session based on the past will help release the tension that created this cycle and ensure we perceive stuff in the moment more clearly.

Here too, recovery from past life can often be very helpful. A past life recovery (also known as past life regression) can get to the anxiety of exploring our memories that can be hidden deep within the individual and collective mind-whether you are actually revisiting a past life, or whether it is more an effective way of digging through "substances" that are deeply held within the energy field and body.

Ultimately, meditations for chakra balancing and toning are effective too. The third-eye chakra's healthy tone is a nasal "AY" and indigo is the balanced hue.

www.ingramcontent.com/pod-product-compliance
Lightning Source LLC
Chambersburg PA
CBHW081419080526
44589CB00016B/2596